Business Guide
to Modern
CHINA

To Hong and Margaret

Business Guide
to Modern
CHINA

Jon P. Alston

and

Stephen Yongxin He

Michigan State University Press

East Lansing

Michigan State University Press
East Lansing Michigan 48823-5202

03 02 01 00 99 98 97 1 2 3 4 5 6 7 8 9

Library of Congress Cataloging-in-Publication Data
Alston, Jon P., 1937-
    Business guide to modern China / by Jon P. Alston and
Stephen Yongxin He.
        p. cm. — (International business series ; # 3)
    Includes bibliographical references and index.
    ISBN 0-87013-423-X
    1. China—Commerce. 2.China—Economic conditions—
1976- 3. Business travel—China—Guidebooks. I. He, Stephen
Yongxin. II. Title. III. Series. International business series
(East Lansing, Mich.) #3.
    HF3836.5.A47 1996
    658.8'48'0951—dc20   96-46475
                                                            CIP

CONTENTS

PREFACE

The motivation to write this book began at Beijing University during 1989, when the senior author was teaching a course dealing with the sociology of work and management. Stephen Yongxin He was then a junior professor and soon became a friend. At that time we began discussing possible research topics for future collaboration. We are most grateful to Beijing University and the College of Liberal Arts at Texas A&M University for developing a program that provided opportunities for international faculty exchanges.

We found that many Americans, and Westerners in general, were ill-prepared to deal with the Chinese mindset, with local Chinese business customs, and with the Chinese society. This society remains largely unknown, even after the gradual opening of the Chinese economy to foreigners over the past twenty-five years.

This ignorance encourages the likelihood of cross-cultural misunderstandings and business failures. The history of China-U.S. business relations offers numerous examples of failures resulting from foreigners' ignorance of Chinese customs, values, and institutions.

In addition, we found that the literature dealing with Chinese business and social practices was either too abstract (aimed at academic audiences) or too specific to provide a foundation for understanding why Chinese managers and officials behave as they do.

These problems encouraged us to write a book that offers practical advice to those wishing to enter the Chinese market as producers or traders; to those who expect to deal with Chinese managers, workers, and government officials; and to students of international business.

We hope *Business Guide to Modern China* provides both practical "how to" advice as well as background information for those who wish to better understand the world's largest society— a society that promises to become a major participant in international business and international affairs in general.

We have relied on the assistance and knowledge of a number of persons, including Qiwen Lu, Naigu Pan, Yongling Xue, Jie Yang, Zhenxing Chen, and Fang Yuan. On the American side, Kerry Cooper of the Center for International Business Studies, Ove Jobring, Paul Parrish, and Dudley Poston were most supportive. Stephen He owes tremendous gratitude to his parents, Changqing He and Shuzhen Wang. Jon Alston remembers his Aunt Edith and his French aunt and uncle and their children and grandchildren.

We also wish to thank the staff of GSU Business Press. In particular, Cary Bynum, director, and Peggy Stanley, managing editor, provided support and much needed editorial skills. This book would not have been possible without them.

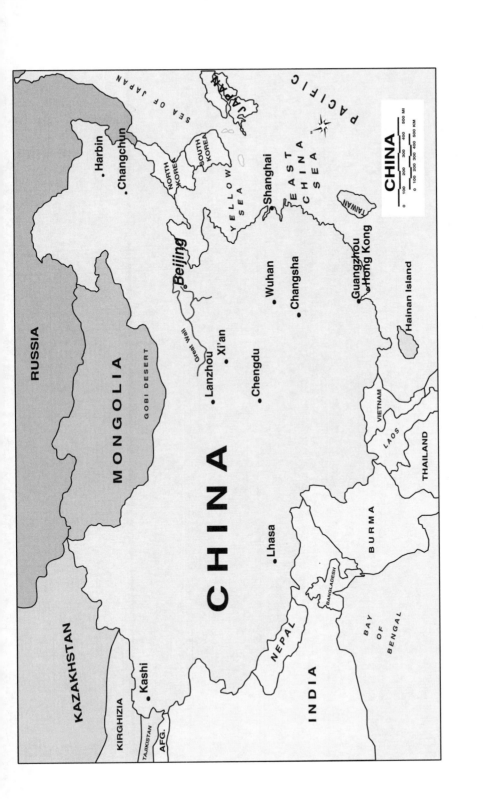

1

Modern China
and Its People

Mao Zedong and the Chinese Communist Party (CCP) came to power in January 1949, after capturing the city of Beijing from the Guomindang Nationalist forces led by Chiang Kaishek. In announcing the establishment of the People's Republic of China, Mao said, "Ours will no longer be a nation subject to insult and humiliation. We have stood up." These words have great significance today for foreigners wishing to do business with the Chinese.

For nearly two hundred years China was dominated and exploited by Western and Asian colonial powers. Even though China now welcomes—in a very ambivalent fashion—foreign business and investment, China's leaders do not ever again want outsiders to gain a permanent or influential position in China's economy. These leaders, now in their sixties and seventies, are sensitive to real and alleged acts that "insult and humiliate" China and its citizens. Foreigners dealing with the Chinese must realize that this fear of foreign dominance remains very real, especially to older Chinese.

A Brief History

Those expecting to conduct business in China should become familiar with some of China's more recent history. Although China's

1

recorded chronology began roughly four thousand years ago, a short review of the last six hundred years provides clues to the modern Chinese national character and to the possible future policies of its leaders.

Early Invasions

The Yuan Dynasty (1279-1368 AD) was established by Mongols, who located their capital in what is known today as Beijing. The Mongols were the first foreigners to rule all of China. Later, the Manchus, also non-Chinese, conquered China and established the Qing Dynasty (1644-1911). Such early invasions made the Chinese fear the outside world and attempt to isolate themselves from foreign cultures.

Western Colonialism and Exploitation

During the early 1800s, the West wanted to obtain tea and silk from China. Unfortunately, the West had relatively little to offer that the Chinese wanted except for cotton and opium, the latter easily available from British India. In 1838 Britain exported to China 40,000 chests of opium, each weighing 133 pounds. In 1839, the Chinese government tried to end the importation of opium, and in June of that year over 2 million pounds of opium were confiscated and burned by Chinese officials. The Western powers resisted these efforts, in large part because the opium trade was highly profitable to the West.

Other colonial powers, such as the Germans and French, used the issue as an excuse to increase their influence in China. The result was the Opium War (1840-42), during which the Chinese forces were decisively defeated. The Treaty of Nanking in 1842 ended the war and forced humiliating concessions on the Chinese, including the loss of Hong Kong and the transfer of five Chinese port cities to the control of British trade interests.

The Nanking Treaty allowed extra territoriality (foreign merchants and citizens were subject only to foreign law) and gave foreigners the right to set import tariffs, which left Chinese industrialization efforts powerless in the face of foreign competition. China was also forced to pay an indemnity for the opium seized and burned, and continuation of the opium trade was essentially guaranteed.

Decline of Qing Dynasty

During the next decades, Western powers and Japan gained more and more control of China's port cities and economy, in part because the ruling Qing dynasty was in decline and relatively power-less. By the 1930s, there were 33 areas (called concessions) in China controlled by Western powers and subject to Western law rather than to Chinese law. Consequently, the Chinese were forced to obey for-eign laws in their richest urban areas, such as the city-ports of Shang-hai and Guangzou (Canton).

Over half of all industrial workers were employed in foreign-owned firms, and Westerners essentially controlled China's export economy. This condition was considered a national shame and is still remembered. Many recent laws governing the activities of for-eign firms in China reflect this historical abhorrence and fear of foreign economic dominance.

As the ruling Qing dynasty weakened during the last half of the nineteenth and the first half of the twentieth centuries, China fell under the control of warring factions and Western forces. This pe-riod of "warlordism" created chaos for most Chinese. In 1911, the Qing dynasty was overthrown by Sun Yat-sen, who attempted to es-tablish a more democratic society. The major goals of the new gov-ernment were to develop an industrialized economy and to estab-lish a central government that would unify China.

After the death of Sun Yat-sen, Chiang Kai-shek became presi-dent of China in 1925, but his party, the Guomindang, was not able to control all of China. In the 1930s, the Chinese Communist Party under Mao Zedong emerged as another threat to China's stability, numerous warlords continued to challenge the legitimacy of the central government, and foreign powers still controlled the economi-cally significant port cities and the economy in general.

Japanese Invasion

Then, in 1931, the Japanese invaded China and soon controlled large areas, including the resource-rich region of Manchuria. Thus, there were three major forces competing to control China: the Guomindang, the Communists, and the Japanese. In addition, local warlords controlled large tracts of isolated areas, while the economy along the coast was dominated by Western powers.

Emergence of Mao and Communist Forces

China continued to be a battlefield during and following World War II. The struggle for control of China continued until Chang Kai-shek was driven off the mainland by Mao and the Chinese Com-munist Party in 1949. At that time, China's economy had been al-most completely destroyed.

The Communist Party, about 1 percent of the 1949 Chinese population, began to rebuild China along socialist lines. Civil order was established, and the economy began to develop. Except for support and aid from Soviet Russia, which ended in 1960, Chinese leaders ignored the West. China became a closed society and to a large extent remains so today.

In 1958, Mao initiated the Great Leap Forward to speed the process of industrialization. Part of the plan was a decentralization of the economy. This attempt was a complete failure, and by 1960 the economy was in near-collapse.

The economy was rebuilt slowly until 1966, when Mao initiated the Cultural Revolution. This was a crusade calling for total equality, during which "superior" persons (intellectuals, teachers, wealthy peasants, managers, and others) were jailed, demoted, tried as "enemies of the people," and often sent to rural areas for years of "reeducation." All things foreign were denounced, and China closed its borders to the outside world. Chinese economy and society stagnated for a decade.

The New Era

When the Cultural Revolution ended in 1976 with Mao's death, China again experienced an economic crisis. The nation had lost much of its economic momentum, and a generation of Chinese was ill-educated, since most schools had been closed for a decade.

In 1976, a new era slowly emerged as economic reforms were instituted. The reforms of the 1970s centered around a limited acceptance of some forms of capitalism and an "open door" policy toward Western knowledge, technology, and investments. This is China's current policy.

It cannot be assumed, however, that the acceptance of limited capitalism reflects a weakening of the socialist ideology. Unlike officials in Russia or Eastern Europe, China's pragmatic leaders do not wish to develop a post-socialist economy. Rather, limited capitalism is seen as a necessary stage on the way to modernization. There is no guarantee that capitalism will be consistently encouraged in the near future, nor is it certain that foreign investment will be encouraged once officials believe that it is no longer needed.

Over the next half decade, Chinese officials expect to invest over US$90 billion in telecommunications equipment. In 1994 China's vice minister Shu Kao-feng announced that China would reduce the number of sanctioned foreign telecommunications suppliers from dozens to three or four in order to increase the competition among foreign companies. Those companies no longer included in the government-sanctioned bidding system will lose their investment in China, though they had earlier been encouraged to enter the Chinese telecommunication markets.

Limited capitalism is seen as a tactic to develop socialism. Capitalistic market mechanisms may be discarded if China's leaders feel they threaten the socialist status quo. Some China authorities, including William H. Overholt, believe that China's economic reforms will inevitably lead to social and political reforms, as happened in South Korea.[1] Thus, foreign investors should be prepared for rapid changes in policy—many to their disadvantage.

Chinese officials' desire to control foreign presence in China was illustrated during April 1994 when taxes on trading profits were eliminated for two years to increase trading on the Shanghai and Shenzhen stocks exchanges. This policy could change overnight should officials feel that trading is too high or that too much speculation is occurring.

China's Economy

The Chinese economy has grown an average of 9 percent a year during the 1980s and first half of the 1990s. The wages of urban workers have tripled in ten years, though some of this advance has been taken away by inflation. According to recent reports, the economy of China is in much better shape than are the economies of Russia and Eastern Europe.[2] During the 1990s, the economy of the Russian republic has declined an average of 10 percent a year, while China's economy experienced an annual gain of 10 percent.

Past government policy, coupled with traditional caution, has encouraged average Chinese to save 40 percent of their income, with an average accumulation of nearly a year and a half of a family's annual income. These savings, of course, might be used either for investment or consumption, depending on the future policies of the central government. We suspect, however, that much of these savings will be used to buy consumer products, making China's consumer markets highly attractive to foreign investors. This high savings level was based in part on the lack of consumer products available to the average Chinese consumer. From any point of view, the economic reforms begun in 1979 have and will create a much better life for most Chinese.

While China's 1.1 billion population is eager for modern goods, the population remains poor. An average family earns less than US$1,000 a year and can buy relatively few products. Products defined as necessities in the West remain luxury goods in China that relatively few can afford.

In the next decade, however, China's people will increase their consumption drastically. Its workers will also produce increasingly more numerous and better-quality goods for export and consumption. There is a great potential in China for the savvy and patient foreign investor.

In spite of many successes, the Chinese economy is inefficient, its factories outdated by twenty years or more, and its workers less productive than those of other industrial countries. China's agricultural workers produce products worth US$228 per person a year, as compared to per capita productivity of nearly US$34,000 in North America, US$18,000 in West Germany, and US$6,700 in Hungary. China's per capita agricultural value is lower than India's (US$358) and Egypt's (US$1,009).[3]

China's economy remained almost totally closed to the West from 1949 until the mid-1970s. For the next decade, foreign business persons dealt only with government officials who served as intermediaries between foreigners and their Chinese colleagues. There was little contact with ordinary people. While the Chinese were eager to deal with foreigners, most contracts were carefully orchestrated by government officials.

During the 1990s, however, some market forces have been allowed to replace political control, though large segments of the economy remain tightly controlled by party officials and bureaucrats. Special Economic Zones have been set aside for economic activities by foreigners, and many cities have streamlined their bureaucratic procedures to encourage foreign investments. This process of decentralization means that foreigners now deal directly with Chinese who may know little about foreign values and ways of behavior.

In addition, foreigners are no longer isolated or protected. Foreigners now face the same problems and frustrations experienced by their Chinese partners. The sudden immersion of foreigners into Chinese society makes it crucial that they understand the Chinese cultural and work environments.

Although China is often thought of as a source of cheap labor and resources, low productivity, increasing taxes imposed on foreign investors, and lack of currency convertibility increase the cost of doing business in China. Furthermore, China is not the easy market for consumer goods from the West that it is sometimes perceived to be. China can produce the latest electronic products and other consumer marvels for its own domestic consumption.

Dealing with Chinese entrepreneurs and officials requires unique talents not always found in the West. Ignorance of these China-West differences will not only increase the already high levels of difficulty and stress of doing business in China, but will also make success less likely.

The Chinese View of Foreigners

The Chinese hold mixed feelings toward foreigners. On one hand, they admire Westerners for their technological knowledge. China's leaders now recognize that much of China's technology lags at least a generation in terms of world-class standards. The Chinese are eager to send students throughout the world—especially to North America—to learn the latest techniques needed to develop a consumer-oriented industrialized nation.

On the other hand, there is an underlying disdain for non-Chinese knowledge and culture. At different periods in Chinese history—the latest being the Cultural Revolution (1966 to 1976)—foreign knowledge was rejected as inferior and anti-Chinese. Foreigners during those times were seen as "barbarians" and a threat to Chinese culture and society.

But now foreigners capable of teaching modern knowledge are welcomed in China. Joint-venture business proposals that include the transfer of technical knowledge are more likely to be accepted than are proposals that involve only economic exchanges, because such proposals offer the greater learning possibilities. A venture that includes the import of the latest technology and extensive training of Chinese workers to use such machinery is likely to be accepted.

A second type of activity encouraged by Chinese officials is the development of tourism, especially if it is in the form of a joint venture with foreign investors. The Chinese recognize that their expertise in tourism is below world standards, and they are eager to learn how to attract tourists. Tourism is seen as a "safe" source of foreign currency, since officials feel that tourists can be isolated in for-foreigners-only facilities away from ordinary Chinese and thus will not, it is hoped, "contaminate" the local population. Also, tourists bring in valuable foreign credits without straining the economy.

Westerners have officially been designated as "foreign friends" and "foreign guests." They can expect to be received warmly by most Chinese, a reflection of both the Confucian value of treating guests with great hospitality and the current official policy.

Westerners walking down a street in any of China's cities will at times be approached by someone who wishes to greet foreigners and perhaps practice English. Foreigners will often be asked to move to the front of the line while shopping or be given someone else's seat in a bus.

Nevertheless, this hospitality is associated with the hope that these strangers will be teachers as well as profiteers. In fact, the Chinese are not especially interested in foreigners making profits from their Chinese ventures. Consistent with the Chinese view of the world in zero-sum terms, there is as yet little confidence that Chinese-foreign business partners can establish a mutual "win-win" relationship. Furthermore, the Chinese have not been completely convinced that profits are legitimate interests for outsiders. This attitude not only reflects Communist ideology but also China's colonial heritage, when Westerners exploited Chinese labor.

Because the average Chinese has been exposed to years of government propaganda stressing the decadence of Western societies, the Chinese are also very curious about Westerners and the West, and foreigners will be asked many questions that to Westerners seem a violation of their privacy. Such questions can be answered vaguely or humorously if they are considered too personal.

Despite curiosity about the West and a respect for the technology it represents, the Chinese proudly believe that their 4,000-year-old culture is superior to others. Furthermore, the Chinese feel they have developed the "correct" standards for social behavior. They judge foreigners by Chinese standards, and consequently—from the Chinese perspective—foreigners can never be completely correct in their behavior. In fact, the Chinese commonly use the term "child-like" to describe Westerners.

The Chinese, however, do appreciate any efforts a foreigner makes to learn about China's culture and language. Foreigners, being foreigners, will be forgiven if they make mistakes in pronunciation or etiquette. Nevertheless, any attempt to "behave correctly" is appreciated and flattering. This is one reason some knowledge of Chinese culture and etiquette is necessary for those planning to work in China or with Chinese nationals. Another reason is that knowledge of Chinese culture and society makes business success more likely.

For thousands of years, the Chinese defined their society as an oasis of civilization surrounded by barbarism. The traditional term for China is the *Middle Kingdom,* or the center of the world. In the Chinese view, foreigners "owe" the Chinese respect and special treatment because of the presumed superiority of Chinese culture. For example, Chinese negotiators often demand advantageous clauses because Westerners owe China some unspecified tribute.

Because the Chinese see China as poor economically but culturally and morally superior, they believe that foreigners from wealthier nations have a responsibility to help China progress materially. For this reason, successful business proposals should be phrased to indicate a willingness on the part of the Westerners to help China's economic development. Being allowed to do business in China is seen by the Chinese as a benefit to the outsiders, even if they gain little monetary profit. Many Chinese officials see the purpose of international business as achieving profits only for China, rather than as a profitable venture for all parties. Foreigners have to be careful that they do not agree to contracts that offer little gain.

General Demeanor and Face

Many Chinese officials, especially those living outside China's major cities, have had little if any contact with non-Chinese. Such persons may rely on rigid protocol to guide behavior, and thus knowing what general etiquette standards guide these officials helps foreigners establish rapport. At the very least, "proper" behavior—or as proper as is possible for a foreigner—relaxes those who are nervous in the presence of foreigners.

Visiting foreigners are at times made to feel superior, especially when Chinese hosts—partly to be polite—praise Western knowledge and claim that China is "backward." Visiting China can become an ego trip for Westerners, but they should be careful not to express any feelings of superiority.

During negotiations, Americans utilize tactics that have been successful in the United States. At times they may use a show of temper or a raised voice to indicate their determination or concern. Americans also use aggressive behavior as a strategy to gain a concession during negotiation by trying to intimidate their business opposites.

Among Chinese, such behavior is taboo and is seldom seen. Strong emotions are usually indirectly hinted at rather than expressed. Losing one's temper is a sign of weakness, and shouting is seen by the Chinese as either an indication of Western feelings of superiority or immature, barbaric behavior.

This sensitivity of the Chinese is linked to a cardinal Confucian virtue of maintaining a serene demeanor. The Westerner who loses his temper loses the hosts' respect and puts into question both the person's sincerity and reliability. Avoid shouting, name calling, and loud criticism at all costs.

The best policy for foreigners in China is to remember at all times that they are guests of the oldest culture in the world and in a nation that has suffered from Western imperialism and colonialism. While the Chinese certainly will not forget the past, they will remember the kindnesses that have been shown by foreigners. The Chinese saying "Use history as a mirror" reflects the importance of the past as a guide and interpretation of the present.

The Concept of "Face"

The Chinese view of foreigners is colored by the major mechanism of social control and social interaction in Chinese society: the concept of *face* or *honor*. The concern for face in Asian cultures is a dominant pattern that increases the differences between the Asian and Western cultures. *Face* is best defined as honor or public reputation. Western equivalents are "good reputation" and "respect." Face is how others evaluate a person. A person who has lost face or has no face receives no respect or consideration from others.

An understanding of face requires the recognition that Chinese morality tends to be situational. A deed or action is not good or bad in absolute terms; it is bad only if it reduces a person's social standing.

There are four dimensions of face: *diu-mian-zi, gei-mian-zi, liu-mian-zi,* and *jiang-mian-zi*. *Diu-mian-zi* means that one's weaknesses are made public; one's shameful or bad deeds are known to others. Note that the embarrassment is not in having done shameful deeds but in losing one's good reputation, or face. The agony is that they are known to others through exposure. It is therefore important behave in ways that others' weaknesses are not exposed (*diu-mian-zi*) in front of others. The Chinese complex protocols of etiquette evolved in part to preserve one's face and to elevate the face of others.

Gei-mian-zi occurs when a person makes others feel respected. Losing *gei-mian-zi* occurs when someone is belittled or insulted by another. One reason the Chinese are so polite to others and so humble when describing themselves is that these behaviors are *gei-mian-zi* (give face) to others.

Liu-mian-zi is face that is developed by avoiding the mistakes of others. *Liu-mian-zi* is given to those whose behavior indicates superior wisdom. This can be achieved by inaction as well as action. This type of face is passive rather than active, since correct behavior in this case lies in not making errors that other commit.

Jiang-mian-zi is a person's public reputation that is enhanced by others. *Jiang-mian-zi* face is increased when you praise someone's talents to a third person. You have increased the first person's reputation. Since the Chinese cannot boast about their own abilities and accomplishments, they rely on their friends to increase *jiang-mian-zi*.

Following this custom, a foreigner should avoid criticizing Chinese. Such behavior decreases a person's *jiang-mian-zi* and makes that individual into a dangerous person. Criticizing others threatens your own reputation and is seen as reducing your *gei-mian-zi* face. In this context, withholding praise is blame enough. Overt criticism destroys the *liu-mian-zi* of your target and weakens your own *gei-mian-nzi* as well.

It is very difficult to get one Chinese to criticize another colleague. Since criticism hurts both parties, direct demands for criticism will be met by embarrassed silence. A "good" person avoids direct criticism. That is one reason why Chinese managers prefer to give bonuses to everyone, irrespective of individual productivity. A worker who does not receive a bonus is essentially being criticized and loses face.

The Influence of Confucianism

Chinese society is organized around the values of Confucianism and continues to be influenced by them, even more than Western societies are influenced by Christianity. Other important value systems form the basis of Chinese national character, notably Buddhism, but Confucianism remains central. The teachings of Confucius (551-479 BC) and his disciples are basic to Chinese social behavior. Confucianism is conservative and resists change. In fact, Confucian values have great inertia, and those who follow this system of values resist innovation and progress. Confucianism forms the bedrock of Chinese society and national character. Even though Chinese Communists have rejected Confucianism, scholars characterize post-1949 China as a neo-Confucian society.

Confucianism is a system of ethics and morals rather than a religion in the Western tradition. The values of Confucianism deal primarily with organization of social relationships, of which there are five major types: ruler and subject, husband and wife, father and son, brother and brother, and friend and friend.

Proper behavior entails duty, loyalty, filial piety, respect for age, and sincerity. These traits must be followed by all persons to preserve social order. When these are rejected, people become selfish and irrational, and chaos emerges. Change disrupts the five major relationships and therefore is rejected.

The ideals of Confucianism are attained in the person of an idealized gentleman scholar living a life of virtue and decorum. Virtuous behavior includes maintaining an innate goodness, love, benevolence, and charity, while accepting the traditional social order.

Proper decorum means following correctly the five social relationships. Confucianism always places the individual within a relationship. Accepting these relationships—being a good brother, husband, or citizen—gives honor to the person. The individual does not exist in Confucianism. A person has an identity only in relation to others—as a daughter, wife, or employee, for example. The quality of a person derives from how these relationships are maintained. All other behavior is seen as either secondary or immoral.

Unlike Buddhism, Confucian values discourage social isolation, since a person who is alone can never live up to the five relationships. There are no Confucian hermits. Some typical Confucian sayings reveal clearly the Confucian philosophy:

- "A good man never lives in solitude; he will always bring neighbors."
- "A scholar who prefers his own ease at home is no scholar at all."
- "A young man's duty is to behave well to his parents at home and to his elders abroad, to speak a few words and be punctual in keeping his promises, to seek the intimacy of the Good. If the young man has done all of that, and has energy to spare, let him study the classics."

According to Confucianism, proper, submissive behavior is preferable to profit-making and business-related behavior. To Confucius, the merchant is opposite to the scholar in character and contribution to society.

Communism has rejected Confucianism though its influence was never totally destroyed. During the Cultural Revolution (1966-1976),

Confucianism was denounced as one of the "Four Olds": old ideas, old culture, old customs, and old habits. Today, Confucianism is tolerated by Communist Party leaders, and Confucian virtues remain models for proper behavior of many ordinary Chinese.

China's Culture

Geert Hofstede has measured cultural differences throughout the world's nations.[4] He uses as his theoretical framework a four-dimensional model of culture that focus on work-related behavior. All cultures, he claims, can be evaluated in terms of four criteria, defined as *power distance, uncertainty avoidance, individualism-collectivism,* and *masculinity-femininity.*

Power Distance

Power distance refers to the degree to which members of a culture accept inequality. High power distance cultures stress large differences between leaders and followers; leaders are different people from subordinates; leaders are entitled to privileges; and everyone has a rightful place in the society that is relatively stable.

The Chinese hold high power distance values. North Americans, Scandinavians, and the British have low power distance scores. In practical terms, business persons from English-speaking nations want to establish equal relations with people they meet, and it is relatively easy for them to establish rapport and informal relationships with strangers. Common American strategies for establishing friendly rapport are to use first names during the early stages of an acquaintance and to assume an informal posture soon after meeting someone. These behaviors are offensive to the Chinese.

The high power distance Chinese maintain formal relations in their business dealings. Furthermore, they do not establish personal relations with people of different ranks. A common complaint of the Chinese is that Americans are too informal and wish to establish informal relations too quickly. For example, Chinese do not call each other by first names unless they are family relatives.

Even colleagues who have worked together for years will use formal titles when they talk. The term "Comrade" is less and less used, and colleagues now call each other by their work titles, such as "Director," or "Vice President." Sometimes both surnames and titles are used, such as "Director Zhou" or "Manager Jiang." "Manager" or "Miss Manager" is as informal as the Chinese wish to be. Those who have advanced academic degrees should be called "Doctor."

A more informal manner of addressing others is to use titles that indicate age. "lao" (old or senior), as in lao-Liu ("senior Liu") is informal and a little slangy, but it also shows respect for age, a central Confucian value. The term "xiau" translates as "young." A young co-worker whose last name is Zhang is called "xiau-Zhang," or "young Zhang." These titles denotes familiarity as well as respect for rank.

In keeping with their emphasis on socially-defined position, high-ranking Chinese officials expect to meet and deal with correspondingly high-ranking foreign executives. This equalizes the power distance involved and shows respect for rank and position. Such meetings may be primarily ceremonial, but not sending high-level Americans to China to meet their Chinese counterparts suggests to the Chinese that the issue is not being taken very seriously by the foreigners.

In high power distance cultures, formal protocols become strict guides for behavior. This includes following official channels. The boss is always right because of the power given that office. Skipping channels to speed communication or improve efficiency is very disturbing to high power distance persons. In China, bypassing officials is seen as insulting behavior and tends to slow down communication in the long run.

Uncertainty Avoidance

The *uncertainty avoidance* dimension measures how comfortable members of a culture are with structured or unstructured situations. Uncertainty-avoiding persons do not like unusual situations, surprises, or being unprepared. Persons from such cultures feel more secure when well-defined rules govern all phases of behavior. Correct behavior means following rules, even when they lead to inefficiency.

It is not surprising that those who have high uncertainty avoidance values also tend to fear the future. To them, the future contains unforeseen events and is therefore threatening. The natural inclination among those who fear future events is to establish as many rules as possible to cover all possibilities.

High tolerance of uncertainty persons prefer few rules to guide their behavior. They wish to remain flexible and can change plans or the direction of their behavior easily and quickly. Such persons do not like to plan future behavior in detail. The future is viewed optimistically, as indicated by the saying "everything will turn out fine." For those who enjoy uncertainty, the future is challenging and exciting, and full of opportunities. Americans usually face future events gladly because their optimism allows them to believe that all future problems can be faced when they occur.

The Chinese, however, fear the future. The Chinese curse "May you live in exciting times" hints at the degree of skepticism and wariness with which the future is viewed. This Chinese attitude toward the future has a number of implications for doing business in China.

Foreigners who bring detailed proposals indicating control of future events will be listened to more closely than those with vague, optimistic plans only sketchily outlined. The Chinese also prefer projects that are characterized as a continuation of the past rather than those that involve a complete break with traditions.

The avoidance of uncertainty on the part of the Chinese is reflected in how Chinese hosts treat their guests. Potential foreign investors enter China only when they have been invited by an organization or group. When an invitation to visit China is made, the sponsors become responsible for these guests. Being a host is a serious responsibility among Chinese.

The Chinese are warmly hospitable. In addition, officials of sponsoring agencies want to account for every minute of the guests' stay. The hosts will have planned a complete set of activities for their guests before arrival in China. A full schedule avoids the embarrassment of uncertainty, controls the behavior of the visitors, and allows the Chinese to be good hosts.

The guests will be met at the airport or train station by the appropriate officials. A round of activities follows. There will be a welcoming banquet the first evening after arrival and an escorted tour of tourist attractions during the first few days. These activities will continue even after business presentations and negotiations have begun.

Many foreigners, still suffering from jet lag, will find it difficult to keep up with this schedule of constant activities. They will not be as alert as usual, and it is common to make costly errors of judgment at this time.

Before arriving in China, experienced foreign travelers try to discover what schedule their hosts have planned—something the hosts may not want to divulge. Experienced travelers will also insist on some "free" time to recover from jet-lag and to orient themselves between meetings. A rule of thumb is to avoid scheduling activities for a day or two after arrival. Visitors are seldom at their psychological and physical best if they try to start full-time negotiations or work duties as soon as they arrive.

On the average, it takes one day after arrival to get over the disorientation of each time zone crossed. Most Americans will need between one and two weeks before they have fully adjusted to China's time zone. Jet lag can be reduced by a stopover in Hawaii or in Hong Kong.

For those unfamiliar with Chinese culture and business practices, a short stay in Hong Kong can reduce the effects of jet lag and offer the possibility of attending seminars on doing business in China. A few days spent learning Chinese business culture and how to live in China can avoid culture shock and misunderstandings when dealing with Chinese.

Once in China, a free day should be included every few days. Such a break gives both the Chinese and their guests time to re-evaluate ongoing negotiations and to change strategies if needed. The Chinese may also want to discuss matters with other officials and department members as well as among themselves.

There should also be periods between formal sessions when no activities are scheduled by the hosts. Otherwise the guests will be forced to discuss business strategies and activities late into the evening. This exhausts the participants and gives the Chinese an added home-court advantage.

Individualism-Collectivism

The *individualism-collectivism* dimension of culture refers to the relative importance of the individual or the group. Collectivist cultures, such as China, integrate individuals into groups. One's identity is derived from group membership rather than from one's own behavior. Collective cultures protect the individual and determine members' behavior and thoughts.

The power of the group is so strong in such cultures that loyalty to the group is defined as more important than efficiency. Since the individual is secondary to the group in such cultures, the individual is encouraged to become emotionally dependent on the group.

By contrast, individualist cultures promote the independence of the person from group ties. Members of these cultures—United States, Canada, France, Australia—expect persons to become autonomous, to value privacy, and to hold private opinions. People are expected to value self-expression and seek self-defined goals.

Foreigners from more individualistic cultures often are unable to understand that decisions and interests in China operate within group or collectivist contexts. Few proposals will be accepted that do not support group interests in some way.

The first act of foreigners is to convince the Chinese that their companies or sponsors are worthy of respect. Since group memberships are paramount in the evaluation of foreigners, representatives of well-known corporations will receive more attention and respect from the Chinese than will those from less-known firms. First communications should include large amounts of information on one's company and its ties to other groups. Requests from those whose group ties are unknown or not respected will be ignored.

Although Chinese culture is group-oriented, as are Asian cultures in general, this emphasis on collectivity does not automatically mean that workers and managers can work together. In fact, Chinese culture is collectivist but not cooperative. It is difficult for Chinese to work well with those outside their groups. Even within groups, individual members may resist working with others for the common good. They will expect, however, for the group to support its members, even if members themselves do not promote group welfare.

Even so, it is much easier in China to convince group members to cooperate among themselves than to cooperate with members of other groups. The primary problem in Chinese organizations is achieving inter-group coordination. This lack of cooperation is disruptive when members of different Chinese government divisions or departments need to work together. Divisions typically do not communicate well with each other, and each will try to maintain as much secrecy as possible. A common complaint of foreigners is the difficulty of getting officials from different departments to agree to support the same policy. Often, foreign businesspersons must separately convince officials in each department to accept a proposal. Thus there can be five sets of negotiations and presentations for one proposal just because the Chinese refuse to coordinate their activities with members of other groups.

Masculinity-Femininity

The *masculinity-femininity* dimension measures how people relate to one another. Masculine countries encourage competition and assertiveness. Success is generally defined in materialistic terms, such as wealth and ownership of things. In masculine societies things are more valued than are people and their feelings.

Feminine cultures encourage cooperative and nurturing types of behaviors. Feminine values encourage interdependence, sympathy with the unfortunates, equality between the sexes, and quality living. Quality of life and concern for people are seen as more important than wealth or ownership of things.

Masculine cultures stress that men should be in charge and define their personalities as naturally assertive. Work is seen as a central activity in life, and success is usually measured in terms of money. Those who become successful by achieving wealth are worthy of respect. The ideal person is ambitious, independent, and work-oriented. Japan, Australia, Venezuela, and Mexico are nations whose members score highest on masculinity values. The Scandinavian nations score lowest in masculinity. China and the United States score in the middle ranges of the masculinity-femininity continuum.

Time and Chinese Culture

Edward T. Hall categorizes how time is used throughout the world into two general systems: monochronic and polychronic.[5] The monochronic time system (*M-time*) is found wherever time is seen as a limited and valuable resource. In such cultures, time units are carefully defined (even to the second) and being on time is a major virtue.

M-time Cultures

Members of M-time cultures are always in a hurry; deadlines are set and must be met. North Americans, Europeans, and Japanese are members of M-time societies. Such persons become nervous and disoriented when valuable time is being wasted, or when goals are not being met. They become frustrated when time is not being used effectively. A Westerner waiting for an hour in a Beijing hotel room for a phone connection is likely to become very frustrated.

M-time people separate duties into discrete units, like beads on a thread. M-time is linear, divisible into discrete sections, and in short supply. M-timers go from one activity to another in a linear, scheduled manner. M-time Westerners work on one "bead," or scheduled business task, then go to the next event when the first is completed.

Schedules are used to sequence activities in a step-like, logical fashion. Meetings may deal with a single topic or an agenda is developed so items can be dealt with in sequence. M-timers may also rank time units according to the relative importance of each task. It is easier for Westerners to agree that one time deserves more attention than another.

P-time Cultures

The second time category is polychronic time, *P-time*, found in most Asian and Latin American cultures. P-time is flexible and changing; schedules are usually ill-defined and ignored when they exist.

Polychronic people see time as a plentiful resource: there is no reason to hurry because there is plenty of time to achieve all goals. Such persons have difficulty keeping appointments, or making detailed plans for the future. As important, P-time is used in many different ways simultaneously: P-timers like to do many things at once. Meetings have few schedules or agendas. Topics are changed or returned to at will.

How P-time Affects Business in China

Because Chinese culture treats time polychronically, Chinese officials seldom feel hurried to complete negotiations and achieve a contract. They prefer to take a long-term view of projects and to plan future events very thoroughly.

A meeting may have many purposes. Some Chinese attending a negotiating session with foreigners may be merely curious about Westerners or may want to practice their English. Others are present because they want to hear what will be discussed just to keep informed. Other purposes at Chinese meetings may be hidden from Western visitors, as when foreigners are asked to visit China to show Chinese the latest technology rather than the real purpose, which is allegedly to develop a joint venture. The foreigner must relax and accept these unofficial complications and interruptions with good grace.

In the same manner, business proposals should have more than one purpose. The Chinese are more likely to accept a proposal if it offers multiple benefits rather than a single but larger benefit. From the Chinese perspective, an ideal proposal is one that brings the nation foreign currency and Western technology, trains the local labor force, and offers a profit as well.

Europe and North Americans (M-timers) find that the pace of activity in China is slow. It may take three to five years or more to complete a proposal or reach agreement. Chinese peasants often plant trees that will not bear fruit for twenty years or more. Chinese business practices also reflect this long-range view of time.

Time is not money in China. Following the Taoist philosophy, the Chinese view time as traveling a circle. They do not like tight scheduling and unilateral deadlines. The slow pace of activities in China is related to the fact that P-time cultures generally do not punish inactivity but do punish wrong action. In the Chinese view, it is much safer to do nothing than to act and perhaps make a mistake.

Americans feel that action is better than inaction ("Don't just stand there—do something!"). Being positive about the future, Americans believe that action results in success and that mistakes can easily be rectified. The Chinese respect action less and feel more threatened by the possibility of being responsible for future errors.

P-time is also flexible and plans are changed easily. P-time is situational rather than linear, so one time unit does not follow another rigidly. For example, when conditions change, the Chinese will want to change contractual agreements or ignore certain clauses.

Planning and Scheduling on P-time

Finally, because time is a plentiful resource, the Chinese do not like to plan ahead in great detail. Nor do they feel comfortable with scheduling events in the distant future. While the Chinese prefer that rules exist to govern all eventualities, they do not feel the need to plan ahead as much as Westerners do, because the Chinese believe that the future, while bleak, is basically ungovernable.

Consistent with this view of time, Westerners should not insist on establishing a strict schedule months ahead of arriving in China. The most effective policy is to state the arrival date and submit a list to your host or sponsor of the persons or official representatives you wish to meet. The schedule may actually be made at the last minute or even after your arrival, but you will see everyone on your list. Let your sponsors make arrangements at their own convenience.

Formal meetings are tightly scheduled. Invitations to such meetings usually announce the length of the sessions, commonly an hour or less. Negotiation sessions can last longer, but even these tend to end at a specified time. It is important not to ignore time limits, since the time of Chinese officials is highly scheduled.

For more informal meetings, especially when the visitor to China is alone, Chinese associates are likely to arrive early for a meeting. There are three reasons for this. First, arriving early is considered a sign of respect, and one gives *face* to the new acquaintance by arriving early. The first meetings between two persons are likely to start early, but after a few meetings, the Chinese will be more punctual.

Second, a person who is alone is seen as lonely and in need of company. This person, it is assumed, wants company and appreciates an early arrival. This is a reflection of the *group* orientation value held by Chinese.

Third, transportation facilities are strained in China. It is hard to arrive at one's destination exactly on time. Low-level representatives travel by bus or bicycle to meet others. If they travel by bus or—in Beijing—by subway, they will almost certainly have to walk long distances and transfer at least once.

In an effort to be on time, a Chinese national may arrive early. He cannot loiter outside or inside a building that houses foreigners. If the weather is uncomfortable, it is easier to enter and arrive early than to walk uncomfortably around until the correct time has arrived. Since there is little concept of privacy in Chinese culture, especially in the Communist regime (privacy is a Western concept and is not valued in China's group-oriented culture), arriving early is not defined by the Chinese as an invasion of privacy.

Foreigners negotiating business proposals tend to be in a hurry. Staying in China is expensive, there are few leisure facilities, and the Chinese pace of business is slower than in "fast clock" cultures such as Germany, Switzerland, and the United States.

Visitors to China usually have only one purpose: to finalize a business deal. By contrast, their Chinese counterparts are dealing with other—often more urgent—issues. Since Americans tend to be impatient to conclude a deal, Chinese negotiators may adopt a slow pace in arriving at decisions in order to gain an advantage. In addition, business negotiations involve political considerations, slow-acting, multilevel bureaucracies, and constant consultations within and among groups. Westerners tend to become very impatient when progress in reaching an agreement is slow—as it *always* is in China.

Westerners are often tempted to extend specific meetings until at least one part of the agenda has been completed. It is common for foreigners to ask for a continuation of a meeting, and for food and drinks to be ordered if necessary. Eating under these circumstances violates Chinese ceremonial functions involved when eating with strangers. The Chinese prefer not to have business luncheons or meeting snacks, though business meals are becoming more common, especially among younger business persons and among close friends involved in mutual business affairs.

Staying for a late afternoon or evening session is even more awkward. Most of the Chinese negotiators do not have telephones in their homes and cannot telephone their families to tell them they will arrive home late. Public transportation will be crowded or the Chinese negotiators may have to bicycle home in the dark. The neighbors and official neighborhood watchers will wonder why someone is coming home so late.

Except for very rare instances, foreigners should keep to their schedules and not try to extend meetings beyond scheduled limits. All-nighters are not a Chinese custom. The solution is to have lots of patience and adapt to China's "slow clock" culture.

Practical Aspects of Chinese Low-level Individualism

As previously discussed, China's culture de-emphasizes the self. The individual is always less important than a group or collectivity. In China, a person is judged more in terms of social characteristics than by individual behavior. Conformity is valued more than personal expression.

Those who conform to group expectations are rewarded by the group's members. As in Japan, conformity in China results in the group's protection and care of its members. People do not prosper unless their groups prosper. This is a motivation for members to support the interests of the group.

A consequence of the *de*-emphasis of the self in relation to the group is that individuals are expected to be humble and never boastful about personal traits or performance. Good manners demand a humble demeanor and self-deprecation. Good qualities should be made public by others rather than by oneself. It is easy for Westerners to misjudge a Chinese if the latter's modest statements about his own talents are taken at face value.

This subordination of self to the group is so pervasive in Chinese society that advertising in China seldom contains claims of product superiority. Advertising messages do not claim that a product is "the best" or is "better than all others." Such messages are offensive to Chinese. Instead, advertisements promote products more subtly, such as indicating that a product "will bring great happiness." Superiority is implied rather than shouted.

Similarly, Chinese applicants should not be asked to promote themselves during interviews. They will automatically demean their qualities and talents. Doing otherwise would be a violation of their moral code, since individual talents should be minimized in favor of the group.

Imagine an interview for a male cook. The applicant will say that, yes, he is a cook, but not a very good one, that he has few skills, and that he may not be able to cook for Westerners. The opposite may be true, but by custom he is not be able to promote himself. These comments should not be taken at face value. The interviewing session will produce few reliable results if the employer expects applicants to promote themselves.

The proper interviewing technique is to ignore verbal denials of talents and to ask the applicant to cook a few dishes. The same person who belittled his skills a few moments ago may prepare excellent dishes from some of the world's best cuisine. Even after the dishes have been served and eaten joyfully, the would-be cook will apologize for the poor quality of the dishes. Verbal denials of skills should be received with suspicion.

While living in a Beijing hotel set aside for foreign professors, the senior author remarked to a school official that the dining hall cooks prepared excellent food, and that even the western style dishes were as good as those found in the West. Both official and cooks never accepted the compliments and kept apologizing for the "inadequate" meals. To acknowledge the well-earned praise would be non-Chinese, though they were privately pleased at being complemented, and the author received more attention afterwards.

Collectivism Extends to Foreigners

The Chinese view foreign individuals as members of groups as well. Foreign guests in China who represent part of a delegation are treated by their Chinese hosts as members of that group rather than as individuals.

The treatment foreigners receive will depend in large part on the prestige of the groups they represent. Showing courtesy to a member shows respect to the employer and the company as a whole. Also, a foreigner may be treated well by Chinese hosts because of past courtesies performed by other members of the same firm. If a former vice-president of a company had hosted an excellent farewell banquet a year ago, the Chinese hosts may feel obligated to reciprocate to a current representative, even if that person were not part of the original party. This courtesy has little to do with that particular vice-president's personal qualities or talents. The Chinese are merely continuing the exchange of courtesies between two organizations.

Foreigners going to China should be aware that their colleagues' past actions, the gifts given and received, and the hospitality exchanged will be remembered. Chinese time horizons may extend beyond the tenure of a number of individuals in the same company, and how one representative behaves has consequences for those who follow. Organizational memory is very long in China.

The representatives from an organization that has displeased the Chinese will receive little respect. As an example, in 1987 the administrators of a Chinese university became angry because they believed that their students attending an American university were being encouraged by American officials to stay in the United States. They could not understand that U.S. university officials did not have the power to force Chinese nationals to return to China after they received their degrees.

About that time, a faculty member from the U.S. university had been scheduled to deliver a series of lectures in China. When he arrived at the Chinese university, his reception was correct but formal. He was told that it was "impossible" to organize students to attend his lectures at that time. A week later, the American was told classroom space could not be found for him, and that perhaps he was too tired to begin his lectures.

Another week later, he was told that a number of students would visit his hotel room to discuss his research, but that formal lectures would be "inconvenient." By this time, the professor realized that there was something he did not understand. He finally got a junior professor to admit to him that he was being isolated to show the hosts' displeasure with his university.

The American professor changed his plane ticket and left two days later. The night before, however, he was given a small farewell banquet as a gesture of respect. The point of this story is that in a collectivist, group-oriented culture such as China, individuals are treated as representative of their groups.

A Chinese host may also suddenly announce that—tomorrow—guests will be escorted to see the Great Wall and the Ming tombs. The host does not understand that the guests may wish to enjoy some free unstructured time to follow their own interests. Coming from a group-oriented culture, the Chinese will assume that personal interests are not important.

The proper policy is to insist that a number of free days be included in the activity schedule. Proper excuses are the need to rest, to meet with colleagues, or to send messages overseas. The hosts will be thankful for such requests, since they don't want to be with the foreigners all of the time either, though they feel obligated to be complete hosts.

Chinese Culture and the Family Group

Chinese culture is family-oriented, and family considerations form the basis for most individual decisions: the family is the most important group membership among Chinese. Each member is expected to develop and maintain a strong sense of loyalty and obligation to the family.

Reflecting the lack of individualism in Chinese culture, children are taught to place family interests over their own. Communist ideology influences the behavior of ordinary citizens less and less, and the family is increasingly providing the framework for morality.

The importance of family relations is seen in the expenditure patterns of families. As family incomes increase, family-related ceremonial expenditures are becoming more common. In spite of official Communist discouragement, more money is being spent on funerals and weddings than was the case a few years ago. Funerals celebrate the respect owed to parents and relatives; weddings celebrate the formation of a new family sub-unit as well as offer participants an occasion to show off their wealth.

In China's rural areas, the peasant family system remained influential during Communist rule, in spite of political rhetoric. Family relations are again emerging as the central form of organization in the countryside. Peasants (farmers) seldom can achieve any form of prosperity unless they are part of various family and kin systems. In some parts of China, the traditional clan system is being reorganized to provide mutual support for their members.

Family members form cooperative networks. Grandparents care for young children and perform household tasks such as meal preparation. In return, younger family members care for older members, since old-age pensions are generally inadequate. Most older Chinese live with their children, and three-generation households are common.

Amoral Familism

In addition, many Chinese follow the practice of *amoral familism*, which is a distrust of all persons except family members. It is assumed that strangers are also interested only in their own family's welfare. Thus, no one can be really trusted except one's family members.

The existence of amoral familism results in rivalries among family groups, usually made up of five hundred persons, or fifteen families or so. An individual without a family to protect him is relatively helpless. The main point of amoral familism is that you must trust your family absolutely and make no assumptions about the possible goodwill or charity of others, except friends and acquaintances with whom interdependency ties have been so well-developed that they can be considered quasi-family members. While family loyalty is a major virtue in Chinese society, there is no single word to denote loyalty to society as a whole.

The Family and the Work Group

Westerners who expect to conduct business with Chinese often ignore the importance of family connections and interests to their Chinese colleagues. The Chinese accept nepotism as moral behavior, since each person has the responsibility of helping relatives as much as possible, even if this means favoritism at the workplace.

S. Gordon Redding has studied the business practices of overseas Chinese living in the Pacific Rim, but outside of China itself, in such places as Hong Kong, Singapore, Taiwan, Indonesia, and Malaysia. He finds that the overseas Chinese are very successful in entrepreneurial enterprises whenever the local government is willing to protect their property and interests.[6]

Redding calls their activities "familial capitalism," in which business activities are directed for family benefits rather than for individual owners. The executives of such firms act as family elders and as the caretaker of family interests.

The Western concept of individualism has led to a preference for impersonal forms of leadership and management. Among the Chinese, by contrast, workers and managers try to expand family-type relationships into the workplace. Leaders are expected to be nurturing, kind, sympathetic, and paternalistic.

Foreigners who have Chinese subordinates will find that they are expected to take an interest in their workers' private lives. The leaders will be expected to take an interest in subordinates' total interests and well-being while maintaining a position of aloofness and reserve, as is expected of family elders.

On the other hand, Chinese subordinates will treat their superiors in ways similar to the ways they deal with their own family superiors. They will offer no criticism or advice, since such actions are considered disloyal to the corporate "family." They will also conform to the leader's wishes and do little that has not been specifically demanded by the leader.

Family considerations form an important dimension along which to develop loyalty and motivation among Chinese workers. Western managers reward workers on an individual basis, such as offering bonuses and pay raises for exceptional work. Such motivational schemes are not as effective in China as they are in the West. Financial bonuses and pay raises are appreciated by Chinese, but there are other, often more productive strategies of motivation.

One successful strategy is to allow subordinates or partners to hire their relatives. Nepotism is a respected and traditional custom in China, and one important benefit of working in contemporary China is the ability to help relatives.

Since relatives trust and depend on each other, relatives in a company form supportive networks. They also provide important connections when favoritism is needed elsewhere. Often, scarce supplies are made available because of family connections. A Chinese colleague will most likely be able to speed up getting licenses and necessary documents when a cousin works in the appropriate government office.

Family ties can also be used to motivate workers to greater efficiency. Often, individual bonuses are heavily taxed or must be "donated" to the company's pension plan. Rewards for exemplary work can take the form of gifts to spouses or relatives. The best worker might be rewarded with a scholarship for a son or daughter; a worker might be given a larger apartment, partially subsidized by the company. A worker who surpasses a production or safety goal might be given certificate for a family meal redeemable in a local restaurant. Western managers must become familial in their behavior to create a better and more effective working climate for their Chinese workers and colleagues.

The Significance of Food and the Family

The importance of family relations is extended into eating and food. The traditional form of greeting among family members and friends is "Have you eaten?" Family meals reflect and support family identity and loyalty. In China, who eats with whom is an important consideration. What is eaten with which person is also significant. Often, a household is defined by those who share a common budget and cook together in the same kitchen. In fact, food is a major expenditure for all Chinese families, irrespective of income.

Families treasure their food traditions, and every family gathering involves eating special foods. Almost all foods have special meanings. Some foods are used to welcome relatives and indicate their visit is a special occasion. Other foods designate rank and family position, and there are foods appropriate for children, for the aged, or for elders and family leaders. Guests are served special food items to show respect to them. Guests are also served first and are often served by the host. Seating for meals is done according to rank, age, and position of those present.

Foodstuffs also have significant symbolic meanings. Almost everything edible has health or medical properties. Even the way food is served has special meaning. Tea brewed in special tea pots made from special clays is considered health-restoring.

Additionally, the close association of food and family has historical origins. Famines and food shortages have been common during China's history, and many adults have experienced periods of severe food deficiencies in the recent past.

In the face of periodic food shortages, the family has been essential in the production of food, in the sharing of food, and in the allocation of food supplies. This has reinforced the traditional centrality of the Chinese family system. One of the reasons for the stability of the Communist regime has been its ability to adequately feed China's population.

Food is therefore an important facet of personal relations. Important ceremonies always involve food as a major part of the celebration. Knowledge of foods and eating protocols is a foundation of proper behavior.

Foreigners in China should become familiar with at least some of Chinese food folklore, since certain foods are appropriate as seasonal gifts. The Chinese are proud of their foods and cooking styles, and they appreciate a guest who takes an interest in what is being served. As it is in France, a little knowledge of foodstuffs is an important part of general etiquette.

Endnotes

1. William H. Overholt, *The Rise of China: How Economic Reform Is Creating a New Superpower* (New York: Norton, 1993)
2. James McGregor, *Wall Street Journal*, 24 September 1991.
3. Yoko Okumura, "The Consumer Market and Market Trends in China," *JETRO China Newsletter* 107 (November-December 1993): 16.

4. Geert Hofstede, *Culture's Consequence* (Beverly Hills, Sage Publications, 1980).
5. Edward T. Hall and Mildred Reed Hall, *Understanding Cultural Differences* (Yarmouth, Maine: Intercultural Press, 1990).
6. S. Gordon Redding, *The Spirit of Chinese Capitalism* (Berlin and New York: Walter de Gruyter, 1990).

For Further Reading

Anderson, E.N. *The Food of China*. New Haven and London: Yale University Press, 1988.

Browning, Graeme. *If Everybody Bought One Shoe: American Capitalism in Communist China*. New York: Hill Wang, 1989.

Li, Jianguo and Diaodui Cheng. "How are Tianjin Families Doing?" *China Today* 10 (October 1990):16-19.

Macleod, Roderick. *China, Inc.: How to Do Business With the Chinese*. New York: Bantam Books, 1988.

McGregor, James. "Hainan Province, Once a Paradise for Capitalism in China, Is Now Lost." *Wall Street Journal*, 23 July 1991, A-13.

Pye, Lucian. *Asian Power and Politics*. Cambridge, Massachusetts: Harvard University Press, 1985.

Seligman, Scott D. *Dealing with the Chinese: A Practical Guide to Business Etiquette in the People's Republic Today*. New York: Warner Books, 1989.

2

◆

Fundamental Conditions
in Today's China

Chinese business, political, and social cultures are in many ways unique among the world's nations. The blending of Chinese and communist structures has resulted in a society that is badly understood by non-Chinese and by Westerners in particular. A major reason for business failures experienced by Westerners in China is their assumption that business can be conducted "as usual."

Although the Chinese welcome foreign investors, and especially foreign buyers and exporters, they do so on *their* terms. The economy and business-related infrastructures of China reflect characteristics that Westerners take for granted, such as a stable and independent legal system, a judiciary that supports contractual agreements, capitalist managerial expertise and ideologies, and the freedom to conduct business without too much arbitrary intervention. For example, in 1994 Chinese officials unilaterally voided a McDonald's Corporation's ten-year lease. Whether the company will be repaid for its forced move to a less desirable location is unclear.

As a result, knowledge of institutions and special economic conditions are especially necessary before conducting business in China or with mainland Chinese. This chapter describes a number of unique features of Chinese society, and the eccentric attitudes and beliefs of Chinese government officials and managers/administrators.

Population

The most dramatic characteristic of China is its population. Despite China's large land area, foreigners are stunned by the density of the people. There are crowds everywhere. China's population today is slightly over 1.1 billion, and will reach more than 1.3 billion by the year 2,000.

China's leaders are determined to reduce the population growth rate. The government encourages couples to have no more than one child; two are sometimes allowed (though not encouraged) if the firstborn is female. Women who agree to sterilization after the birth of the first child are given bonuses. Couples who agree to limit their families to one child are given preferences for housing, pay raises, and better health care, and they also receive higher retirement benefits.

Currently, China's population is increasing approximately 1.4 percent a year—a rate that is low for developing countries. Even so, an estimated 17 million Chinese are born each year, enough to replace the entire population of Tokyo or New York.

Providing for a billion-plus persons strains China's economy. Since 1982, China's population has increased by 125 million, the equivalent of Japan's current population or almost half the population of the United States. The employment of an ever-increasing number of adults has become a major concern of China's leaders and is central to all economic plans and activities.

In spite of the population growth of recent decades, China's food supply comes from essentially the same amount of tilled acreage available a generation ago. Little unused fertile land is available for additional agricultural purposes. In fact, the total acreage devoted to agriculture decreased slightly during the 1980s. Some agricultural acreage changed to industrial use, some was used for new housing, and some was lost through soil erosion.

Only about 30 percent of China's land area can be cultivated. The rest of China's geography is made up of deserts, grass plains, or mountains. However, the available agricultural lands are very rich, allowing for high productivity. Such lands are concentrated in the valleys of China's largest rivers, especially the Yellow, Yangtze, and Pearl rivers.

Agricultural areas are found in the east and south, and along the coast. As a result, the population is concentrated in those areas, while huge tracts that are essentially uninhabitable or not conducive to agriculture are left virtually empty. Yet the population has been increasingly better-fed through more intensive and efficient use of the land. The increased per-acre yield over the last decade or so is a monument to Chinese hard work and ingenuity. Unfortunately, the need to feed, house, and, in general, support an increasing number of persons has placed great pressures on China's environment.

China suffers extensively from decades of neglect of environmental issues. Large areas of China have become polluted and their forests destroyed by acid rain and destructive lumbering practices. In the northwest, there has been increasing soil erosion and desertification. Major lakes and rivers are also polluted. China's major cities, such as Beijing and Shanghai, are also severely polluted. The air quality in the major cities is among the worst in the world.

China's government has taken heroic measures to increase the quality of life, life expectancy, and the general health of its people. Whether conditions can continue to improve depends in large part on China's ability to develop an import/export-oriented economy and train its workers to manufacture and use the latest Western and Pacific Rim technologies.

For these reasons, China's leaders have been willing to open the borders to foreign business. How much liberalization and openness the leaders are willing to allow is uncertain. Nevertheless, foreign businesspersons and their investments will remain welcome to some extent throughout the 1990s.

Ethnic Groups

China's population is extremely homogeneous, with about 93 percent of Han origin. The Han originate in the Great Yellow Plain, China's richest agricultural area. The Han people founded the Han Dynasty, which lasted from 206 BC to AD 220; Chinese national character and culture derive from the Han civilization.

The remaining 7 percent of the population consists of various minorities called *National Minorities*. There are 54 officially designated minorities, plus a small number that have not been officially defined as cultural minorities. Most live in the frontier and border areas in fairly isolated regions.

In the past, Chinese officials have attempted to incorporate these minorities into the Han population and culture, in part by moving Han members into areas where minorities live. The current policy is to respect local cultures and customs, and most minority groups have maintained large portions of their traditional culture.

Many minorities are Moslem and are the groups most likely to resist cultural assimilation into the Han majority. Others, such as the Tibetans, have also strongly resisted the forced assimilation policies of the Communist regime. Some groups are Turkish in origin. Most members of these groups are herders of sheep, goats, camels, and cattle and resist modernization, which would involve giving up their nomadic life to settle in urban areas.

Great cultural variations, as well as major language divisions, also exist among the Han from region to region. The Han Chinese have adopted Mandarin from the north as the official language of China. There are seven other Han-related languages each spoken by at least 10 million persons. These dialects are different enough so that most are not mutually understood without study. The ethnic and regional variations in the Chinese population may in the future result in domestic conflict, thereby increasing the difficulty for foreigners to successfully invest in China.

Physical and Economic Geography

The People's Republic of China encompasses 9.6 million square kilometers (almost 3.7 million square miles) and extends roughly 4,000 kilometers from north to south and 4,800 kilometers from east to west. This area forms the second largest nation in the world, after Canada, and is roughly the same size as the United States or Western Europe.

China leads the world in both coal and iron ore reserves. Coal, China's major energy source, is found primarily in northern China, such as in Shanxi Province, where China's highest quality coal is located. China's transportation system is antiquated and inadequate, and only a small portion of the coal mined can be transported to the south and southeast, where industry is concentrated.

China also has large petroleum reserves in ten oil fields. Recent exploration discoveries in coastal waters will make more petroleum-based energy available to local industries. A plan exists to develop China's offshore oil reserves primarily for export purposes. Industrial energy needs will be met in part by nuclear plants now under construction.

China claims to have one of richest hydropower resources in the world, although hydroelectricity is not yet a significant source of energy because large water flows are generally located far from population and industrial concentrations. A number of large hydroelectric projects are under construction, including the very ambitious Sanxia Project on the Yangtze River, but hydro-energy will remain a relatively minor source of power in China for the next several decades.

China also contains large mineral reserves, with more than twenty rated among the largest in the world. Most reserves are located in the eastern half of the nation and are generally undeveloped. Prospecting is being conducted in the west and the northeast, and such efforts should discover additional reserves.

Climate

Because of the country's large size, China's climate is varied. Six broad temperature zones run north and south and range from tropical to cold-temperate. January is generally the coldest month, and July, the hottest.

Each year from October to March, cold, dry winter winds blow from Siberia through the Chinese mainland. They cause severe cold and dry winters in much of China except in the southernmost region. From April to September, eastern China is dominated by a warm, humid air stream from the Pacific Ocean, bringing high temperatures and rainfall.

Wide variations of climate from region to region cause an unbalanced distribution of population and economic activities. Of the slightly over 1.1 billion people in China, more than 90 percent live in the eastern half of the country, leaving the rest essentially uninhabited. Industrial activity is concentrated in the eastern regions, primarily in Shanghai, Beijing, Tianjin, and Liaoning Province.

Agriculture is also concentrated in a limited area, as previously mentioned. The northwestern area, comprising half (52 percent) of China's land area, contains 4 percent of the population and 7 percent of its farmland. In contrast, the southeast constitutes 48 percent of the land area and 93 percent of the farmland. This area is called China's granary because of its high grain production.

Economic Divisions

Chinese economic planners have divided China into six economic divisions, each subdivided into provinces, autonomous districts, and metropolises. These divisions are economically and culturally dominated by one or two urban centers (see Exhibit 2-1).

Of the six divisions, eastern China is the most developed and wealthiest, and contains the largest concentration of industry. Most of China's modern machinery and consumer goods are produced in this area. However, the area is poor in energy sources and obtains coal and petroleum from the North. The eastern area's farm output is the largest in China, due to the heavy rainfall the area receives.

Northern China contains more than 70 percent of the nation's coal, the country's primary source of energy. Its iron ore deposits are the second-largest in China. Most of China's steel and chemical plants, textile mills, and machinery production are concentrated in this area. One-fourth of China's steel and one-half of its automobiles are produced in northern China.

South-central China has experienced the largest economic growth because economic reforms have been concentrated in this area. Guangdong Province has attracted investment from Hong

Exhibit 2-1. China's Economic Divisions

Division	Main Sub-Units[1]	Central Cities[2]	Capital Cities
North	Beijing, Hebei, Tianjin, Shanxi, West Inner Mongolia	Beijing, Tianjin	Shijazhuang, Taiyuan, Hohlot
Northeast	Liaoning, Jillin, Heilongjiang, East Inner Mongolia	Shenyang	Harbin, Changchun
East	Shanghai, Jiangsu, Zhejiang, Anhui, Jiangxi, Fujian, Shandong	Shanghai	Nanjing, Hefei, Hangzhou, Jinan, Fuzhou, Nanchang
South Central	Henan, Hubei, Hunan	Guangzhou, Wuhan	Shengzhou, Changsha, Naning
Southwest	Guandong, Guanxi	Chongqing	Chengdu, Lhasa, Kunming, Guiyang
Northwest	Shanxi, Gansu, Qinghai, Ningxia, Xinjiang	Xian	Lanzhou, Xining, Yinchuan, Urumqi

[1] Cities, autonomous districts, or provinces
[2] Not including central cities

Kong, and its GNP has doubled twice in the last fifteen years. South-central and eastern China are the areas where most foreigners locate their businesses.

The northwest division occupies 32 percent of China's land area and contains 7 percent of its population. The weather is extremely arid and land use is primarily grazing.

China's Special Economic Zones

China has established special economic zones (SEZs) to encourage foreign investments (see Exhibit 2-2). These zones permit more privatization and capitalist ventures than are allowed in the rest of China. The SEZs are also designed to contain and control capitalist ventures. If they develop to the satisfaction of China's leaders, then the SEZs will increase in size and number, and selected capitalist practices, such as foreign ownership of land, will also be expanded to other areas of China. Capitalist practices will be accepted only if they are deemed successful experiments in the SEZs and do not threaten socialist ideology.

The locations of China's SEZs provide foreign investors with easy access to mainland China. Four SEZ cities are in the south, near Hong Kong. Other SEZs are located adjacent to Macao and Taiwan.

Exhibit 2-2. Socioeconomic Data for China's Special Economic Zones, 1990

	Shenzhen	Zhuhai	Shantou	Xianmen	Hainan
Population[1]	1,020	190	60	370	6,540
Size[2]	327.5	121	57	131	34,000
Value of Exports[3]	2.8	.49	.42	.77	.41
Number of foreign enterprises	75.7	411	174	272	220
Amount of foreign investments[4]	.67	.30	.15	.51	.16
Total industrial value[5]	**16.0**	**4.0**	**1.5**	**6.5**	**2.8**

[1] = In 1,000s
[2] = In square kilometers
[3] = In billion yuan
[4] = In U.S. billions
[5] = In billion yuan

Source: Huang Taihe, "Development of China's SEZ," Beijing Review, April 8-14, 1991

The original SEZs are also coastal ports that were responsible for most of China's international trade before 1979.

The opening up of the SEZs to foreign trade indicates more than a desire to encourage foreign investments. China suffers from a scarcity of raw materials, in part because of its inadequate transportation system. Chinese officials hope that the SEZ port cities will encourage foreigners to import raw materials, which will then be processed by local labor and exported throughout the world.

Special Economic Zones developed from the theory of the "great international cycle" proposed by two Chinese economists in 1987 and presented to the Thirteenth Party Congress. This theory, based on the need for China to build a modern economy and find work for surplus labor in the agricultural sector, proposed that excess agricultural laborers be transferred to coastal cities where, with foreign capital and technology, they would work in labor-intensive industries. The result would be the manufacture of export goods, the integration of China into international trade networks, and the utilization of surplus labor.

At that time, labor-intensive industries, such as electronics, steel, and textiles, were being transferred from the more advanced industrialized nations to the developing and underdeveloped economies. China's leaders hoped to take advantage of this shift of industrial production by providing cheap labor in exchange for foreign investments and technology. The resulting products would be exported in exchange for foreign currency, which would then be used to modernize China's industries by buying foreign technology. Thus China would enter the "international cycle," use surplus labor to earn foreign credits, and modernize at the same time. This strategy is essentially the one used by Asia's new economic miracles of Japan, Taiwan, Singapore, Hong Kong, and South Korea.

The plan suggests that the types of foreign investment that will be welcomed are those that are export-oriented rather than those that attempt to enter China's consumer markets. These firms would use imported resources, thereby reducing pressure to produce local materials, which in any event would also strain China's inadequate transportation infrastructure. The concept of an "open door" to foreign involvement in China's economy will remain restricted mainly to the export sector. The exceptions, such as Kentucky Fried Chicken outlets in Beijing, will most likely remain exceptions.

The advantages of SEZs for foreigners is that local governments are encouraged to streamline bureaucratic procedures, reduce red tape, and maintain flexible rules. The provincial governments have eased land-leasing requirements, built superior transport and power facilities, and relaxed hiring and firing policies. The strictures against certain leisure activities, such as nightclubs, have also been relaxed, so that foreign workers have more entertainment facilities available to them than is the case in other parts of China.

Three SEZs are in Guangdong, the province where Guangdong City (Canton), is located. Like Shanghai, these areas have always been trade areas and relatively Westernized. Xianmen is also highly commercialized, and government officials in these two provinces are eager to attract foreign investors. For a number of years, Hainan successfully attracted the highest amounts of foreign investments, and officials developed a number of capitalist measures to attract foreign investors and encourage the economic development of the SEZ.

Other areas equivalent to SEZs are generally urban regions in which the municipal government encourages the location of foreign investments. The city of Shanghai and its surrounding areas eagerly seek out foreign investors and buyers.

Decentralization of Power

China's leaders have attempted to modernize their economy through a process of decentralization, thereby allowing more officials—especially those at provincial and municipal levels—the authority to make economic decisions. At the same time, however, decentralization was accompanied by maintaining overlapping responsibilities among various governmental divisions. The policy of overlapping powers reflects the desire among central authorities to maintain central control and to keep lower-level officials weak, since few can make unilateral decisions.

Victor Chou, a Hong Kong legal professional, states that approval to invest in a state-owned enterprise demands a least the support of a dozen ministries or bureaus. Officials are attempting to streamline various bureaucratic procedures, but progress is limited. Foreign entrepreneurs must negotiate with each bureau until all appropriate officials sign an agreement. Some officials are more eager than others to cooperate, and most do not communicate with one another. These patterns of ambiguity and overlapping authority form day-to-day hazards for foreign investors.

The effort to encourage profitability through more local autonomy has had a number of negative as well positive consequences.

Decentralization has given more power to provincial and municipal authorities, and it is possible to make some decisions without involving Beijing officials. However, local governments have also taken advantage of their new freedoms to protect their immediate markets and interests.

For example, more local authorities are erecting tariff barriers to decrease competition for their own industries. In Heilongjiang Province, officials placed an absolute ban on the importation of thirty categories of goods, plus tariffs on over one hundred other products. Some provincial governments have placed tariffs on beer, tobacco, textiles, and washing machines. Scarce raw materials at times cannot be transported outside the area, but must be processed within the province.

Shanghai municipal government officials station armed police at the city's entrances to guard against those who wish to take advantage of Shanghai's export laws. If outsiders from other provincial units wish to enter Shanghai, they must pay a special "tax." Many of these manufacturers are foreigners. This causes unanticipated costs for export/import-minded foreigners. West of Beijing, provincial leaders at one time did not allow trucks loaded with coal to travel on the province's highways unless the mining company paid a transport fee. This tax was eliminated when mining directors complained to higher authorities in Beijing.

It is difficult to establish cost projections when local taxes are unexpectedly imposed on a product being exported or imported. While such taxes are usually rescinded when foreigners complain to central authorities, these appeals take time, and the resulting delays can be costly.

This trend toward regional autonomy resembles to some degree the "warlordism" existing during most of the first half of this century in China. If this trend continues, foreign investors may find it increasingly difficult to sell consumer goods and to obtain raw materials without paying high premiums that are not imposed on local buyers.

Inside/Outside Economies

Foreigners wishing to invest in Chinese ventures face two vastly different economies, called in Chinese *jihua nei/wai* (inside/outside economies). The first economy is state-run. It is made up of large enterprises such as steel works, automobile manufacturing complexes, or electronics manufacturers. These are managed by government officials, are part of five-year plans, and follow government policy.

For the most part, the functions of state-run enterprises are to serve political and national goals rather than economic goals. These businesses must produce whatever goods a central authority has decided should be made available. The firms provide employment irrespective of labor needs. A majority of state-owned enterprises operate at a loss, and roughly half of their workers are redundant.

The state-run economy follows five-year planning rather than the market-driven rules of supply and demand. Its products are sold at state-run stores. These enterprises were developed along a Soviet-style model prevalent in Russia before the 1980s. Many older executives received training in Russia or from Russians sent to China as teachers. Today, Chinese students are encouraged to attend universities in the United States and elsewhere, and visiting scholars are welcomed in Chinese universities and institutes, but an older generation of administrators and managers who are unfamiliar with capitalism exists.

State-run firms are allocated predetermined amounts of supplies and materials at below-market prices. The companies are then expected to produce "X" amount of products. Their products are bought at government-dictated prices and sold in state-run stores at official, generally subsidized, prices. The firms are given priorities to receive foreign currencies with which to buy and import the latest high-tech equipment. Most of these enterprises operate at a loss and are extremely inefficient.

The second economic sector is more loosely controlled by the central government, and more closely follows free-market mechanisms. This "outside" economy is dynamic and has provided most of China's economic growth and development for the last decade or so. The outside sector consists of small and medium-sized enterprises, those not run by state officials, and those established and managed by entrepreneurs with an average enterprise labor force of five or less.

According to James Steepen, who was resident manager in Beijing for a U.S. multinational firm, these outside enterprises offer foreigners the greatest opportunities for joint-venture partnership.[1] Many are located in China's free economic zones, where foreign ventures are encouraged and where government restrictions and red tape are at a minimum.

We advise foreigners wishing to conduct business on a long-term basis to seek out the "outside" sector. These firms are part of the "responsibility" system and are concerned with profits. Their managers and workers are eager to do business with foreigners.

What Chinese Officials Want From Foreigners

Officials favor proposals to export made-in-China products and to upgrade workers' skills. Foreigners who wish to invest in new factories and import the latest technology in order to produce goods for exports have the highest likelihood of acceptance.

The Chinese are eager to learn how to operate the latest technology. Almost all joint ventures with foreigners include a provision for the training of local workers. The rationale of this policy is that, in the future, the Chinese will be able to match or surpass Western technical knowledge. Westerners need to realize that Chinese officials believe Westerners' presence in China is temporary—*temporary* meaning ten, twenty, or fifty years or more.

This policy of learning from (and later discarding) foreigners was adopted by the Japanese during the nineteenth century. The Japanese were willing to hire large numbers of foreigners and to send their own citizens to study and observe in foreign countries.

Like the Japanese, the Chinese are reluctant to open their national markets to foreign interests. Money is made by entering the U.S. market, and the Chinese are eager for help to sell to Americans, but they remain extremely suspicious of becoming dependent on foreign manufactures. This policy has been extremely successful, with the result that China-U.S. trade runs a deficit in favor of China. The U.S.-China deficit in 1994 was slightly over $30 billion. The U.S.-China deficit is second to that of the U.S.-Japan deficit, and accounts for 20 percent of the total U.S. trade deficit.

Trade opportunities for American companies to enter and sell in China's domestic market remain extremely limited, although a few consumer products have been allowed into China. Kentucky Fried Chicken, Pepsi Cola, Apple Computer, and McDonald's have become symbols for Western penetration, but such successful consumer-oriented ventures are limited. The Chinese do not yet have many surplus economic resources, and most Chinese will not be able to buy great amounts of foreign goods. Further, China's leaders seek to strengthen the economy in order to be *independent* of foreign influences, not to *join* the global economy (see Exhibit 2-3).

Exhibit 2-3. Direct Foreign Investment in China

	1991		1993[1]	
	Number of projects	Value (US$ in thousands)	Number of projects	Value (US$ in thousands)
Hong Kong	8,502	7,215	9,758	15,881
Taiwan	1,735	1,389	2,073	2,130
United States	694	548	1,111	1,209
Japan	599	812	567	459
Singapore	169	155	244	413
Thailand	52	108	178	238
South Korea	230	137	277	193
Total	12,978	11,977	17,981	25,293

[1] *January-March*
Source: *JETRO China Newsletter* 109, March-April 1994, 16

Politics Versus Business

A major barrier to economic development in China is the traditional antibusiness attitude of the Chinese, who have always held business in low regard. For the last two thousand years, power and honor were given to those who passed the national examinations and became the higher-ranked bureaucrats. The knowledge being tested in these examinations was that of the Confucian classics. Practical knowledge, whether military- or business-related, was scorned by China's rulers, nobility, and intellectuals.

Linguistically, the term "business" *(shang)* has negative connotations, including the concepts of selfishness, greed, and having no compassion *(wuqing)*. Many Chinese today condemn those who have ambitions to become wealthy or successful in business as being *wuqing.*

China's leaders realize that further economic development necessitates more freedom in the economic sectors. Yet each liberalization is often followed by a retrenchment, as the elites perceive that economic freedom may impose similar changes in the political arena. This politics-versus-business conflict results in arbitrary cancellation of policies and contracts as political and economic conditions change.

Foreign investors face the threat that political considerations will reduce the economic liberalization movement that began in 1979. Foreigners should not assume that current agreements are iron-clad and unalterable. Civil contracts are powerless in the face of changing political interpretations.

A recent report describes the economic status of Hainan Island in Southern China.[2] Hainan became a province in 1988 when the government established it as a laissez-faire economic area for national and foreign investors. One attraction of the area was that exporters could keep 96 percent of the foreign currency they earned. When profits soared two years later, the Beijing tax collectors reduced that margin to 80 percent. The rationale was that too much profit was antisocialist and that profits should enrich China rather than outsiders.

In another example of political interference in Hainan, a Japanese-owned development company signed a contract with Hainan authorities to develop 100 square kilometers, including building a seaport, a power plant, and roads. Soon after the agreement was signed, however, a new and more politically conservative administration came into power, and the company's officials were told that they could develop only 6 square kilometers.

Chinese Bureaucratic Values

The motto of the Chinese bureaucrat should be "He who does nothing cannot be blamed." This two-thousand-year-old bureaucracy was established primarily to control the population. The goal of this control was to maintain the social status quo to the advantage of the ruling classes.[3]

The same ethos is prevalent in contemporary China—bureaucrats protect themselves from errors and changing policy by being responsible for as little action as possible. The purpose of the system, in both its ancient and modern forms, is to discourage innovation. A consequence of this mindset is that every decision, no matter how trivial, is referred up the bureaucratic structure as far as possible. In this way, lower-level officials cannot be blamed for wrong decisions or actions that they did not develop.

A generation of older Chinese remembers the violent changes in policy during the Cultural Revolution (1966-1976). During the 1950s, many scholars were encouraged to learn and teach the Russian language. Soviet Russia was China's friend and economic sponsor. When China rejected Russia's "friendship" and the Cultural

Revolution began in 1966, all teachers of Russian were denounced as Russian spies or at least as having been "politically tainted" by their foreign knowledge.

These "criminals" were sent to rehabilitation camps or rural communes to "learn peasant ways." After spending six months in jail, one teacher of Russian and English worked in a pig farm for three years. He was rehabilitated only when government officials decided that English-speaking workers were needed.

Such experiences were typical of millions of Chinese. Those over fifty remember the events of the Cultural Revolution and fear any change of policy that might once again disrupt their lives. Consequently, that generation prefers to do nothing rather than to risk punishment.

In this light, decisions will be made either by the highest official possible or by a group of some type. If by the latter, no one can be blamed for showing initiative. This is one reason Chinese work groups, negotiating teams, and similar organizations are larger than those found in the West. It is harder to pinpoint individual activities in large teams. The Chinese have further blurred accountability by overlapping responsibility. That is, every action usually is the province of at least two or three bureaucratic structures.

Chinese Law

From a Western perspective, China has no legal system. Instead, behavior is guided by administrative fiat, which can change at any moment. Any legal statement can be ignored or changed according to changes in policy, ideology, or the personal whim of officials.

Contractual Agreements and the Law

Foreign businesspersons find that contractual clauses can be rejected by Chinese officials when such clauses are no longer useful and original conditions no longer exist. Officials who disagree with a law often ignore it or subvert it completely, since some laws are merely showpieces and are not to be taken seriously. Laws will be enforced only if and when it suits those in power. Bureaucrats find it easy to adopt a wait-and-see attitude toward laws they do not favor.

Contractual agreements in China are tentative rather than absolute. Furthermore, persons who enforce a law that is discarded because of changing political attitudes or shifts in the balance of power are held responsible for their actions. That is, the enforcement of a law that liberalizes local investment may result in demotion or worse if politically conservative leaders regain their former levels of influence.

Obscurity and the Law

It is sometimes difficult to determine if a law exists. Chinese officials are extremely hesitant to give out information or legal opinions, especially in writing. As an official once told a foreigner who asked to obtain a copy of certain laws, "Foreigners don't need to know about approval procedures. We have special work units that deal with foreigners." In fact, knowing legal statutes too well may indicate that the foreigner has illegally obtained "secret information." Even telephone directories were considered state secrets a few years ago. This tendency to restrict information is slowly being eroded, but it remains strongly entrenched.

It is difficult to determine if a statement is, in fact, a law. Many administrative announcements may be "guidelines" rather than absolute demands. Others are trial balloons to test the relative power of one or another political faction.

In addition, most government publications are still defined as state secrets. Their circulation is almost always restricted, including procedural guidelines and laws. Even officials in one office may not be aware of laws promulgated by another division.

Government Officials Versus Legal Specialists

The Chinese legal system is supported and interpreted by government officials and bureaucrats rather than by legal specialists. Since all laws are administrative statements, laws are the responsibility of specific administrations and ministries. The administrative nature of China's legal system is indicated by the fact that there are few lawyers in China. Shanghai, a city of twelve million and China's commercial center, has only three hundred full-time lawyers.

During 1986, a foreign negotiating team was told that a law existed limiting the value of the technology contributed by a foreign partner to no more than 20 percent of the company's equity contributions. This statement could not be found in published statutes. Members of a U.S. embassy eventually discovered that the 20 percent limit was an "internal guideline" independently issued by a department.

Legal Experiments

Officials also promulgate laws as experiments. Laws are passed whose purpose is to see if they are effective. If they are, then these legal statements become more permanent. A few years ago, the city of Shanghai was allowed to have a stock exchange when city officials pushed for its establishment. A few months later, however, conservative officials became alarmed when they realized that (1) some persons began to concentrate wealth through stock speculation, and (2) stock liquidity demanded that stocks be bought and sold as individual property—of which there is little in China. Government officials have restricted the activities of Shanghai's stock exchange, although the "experiment" continues. Beijing officials still decide which companies will be listed on the Shanghai exchange.

Each regional district contains unique rules governing foreigners' business activities. They are often contradictory due to the varying degrees of conservativeness of local officials. Local officials who have close relationships with Beijing administrators also enjoy a greater latitude to act and innovate or to ignore selected laws and administrative "guidelines" than do those who lack influential sponsors.

Laws in the Western tradition are being developed in modern China to guide commercial dealings. Few laws regulated business before the early 1980s because business was defined as an extension of social relationships. Business is nevertheless still largely based on personal connections, the exchange of favors (*guanxi*), or negotiation.

A few years ago, a number of foreign firms were told by Chinese officials that their taxes were being been arbitrarily increased. The rationale was that "unjustified profits are illegal." The foreigners began to negotiate with representatives of appropriate bureaus (discovering who they were took time), and U.S. Consulate officials were called in to protest. Eventually, most of the increase was eliminated as being the result of "unwarranted zeal" of unnamed officials. Foreign managers who had close ties with the right Beijing officials were able to ignore the increase completely.

Ambiguity of the Legal System

Two general sources of confusion exist when foreigners deal with the Chinese legal system. The first has already been mentioned: the often rapid changes in the laws themselves. Enforcement and interpretation can change without notice, and new directives are enacted overnight.

The second source of confusion lies in the fact that many bureaucrats fear that enacting or enforcing certain laws might someday create problems for their careers. As a result, many directives are incompletely publicized and kept semi-secret, while others remain closely held secrets. This is especially true with laws that go counter to socialist values but are needed to develop a more market-driven economy.

In 1992, Beijing officials informally passed the word that foreigners would be allowed to gain at least minority control of selected state-owned and state-operated collectives. The privatization of such firms runs counter to socialist ideals, though the firms' investment structures form a capitalist-socialist compromise. The plan essentially proposed the sale of state assets to foreigners.

Conservative officials define the taking of profits from these collectives by foreigners, even if they invest in capital improvements, as a direct loss of Chinese resources and wealth. Allowing foreigners to be part-owners of these collectives violates socialist ideals as well as reduces the probability that China can maintain an economic and ideological independence from foreigners.

No one knows yet if this proposal to privatize state firms will become general policy, thereby allowing unrestricted investments on the part of foreigners. The chances are that a few collectives will be made available to potential foreign investors to see if this experiment becomes successful. Until then, the plan will be kept semi-secret, and potential investors will be carefully selected.

This suggests that close ties to appropriate officials are necessary, and that some foreigners will be favored over others. The ambiguity of China's legal system demands that potential investors develop informal links with the correct officials.

Social Control In China

The preference for group identities, such as the family, results in a society that forces all persons into tightly-knit webs of relationships. The most important of such networks are the work team and the neighborhood committee.

The Small Work Team

All persons involved in any activity outside the home are members of small work teams (*xiaozu*), usually consisting of eight to fifteen co-workers. These groups are found in schools, factories, offices, penal institutions (inmates and guards separately), and neighborhoods. *Xiaozu* are based primarily on work-related ties. These groups hold regular meetings so that the members can receive messages from the central government and study required political materials.

Each group elects a leader who reports to appropriate party officials. The *xiaozu* was established to weaken the role of competing group relationships such as family groups, merchant organizations, and labor unions. It also directly ties each individual into a national system of observation and political control. These groups meet several times a week if necessary.

The significance of such groups for foreigners is that the *xiaozu* are influential agents of social control. Their demands supersede local demands made by foreign employers. A factory *xiaozu* is allotted space and time for study and discussion. If there is a conflict between work and the group's demands, the latter prevails.

Foreigners need to learn to work with these locally based *xiaozu* networks. Their leaders are influential and must be taken into account. A foreign manager wishing workers to work overtime or to be more concerned about quality must go through these work groups.

The *xiaozu* are also important as sources of motivation, and it is often necessary to deal with workers as members of these groups. Production prizes and bonuses often will be more effective when they are awarded to the *xiaozu* rather than to individuals. An appreciated prize is a banquet given to all members of the group being rewarded.

On the other hand, a worker with a grievance will communicate his complaints to the *xiaozu*. The other members usually will support the complaining member (rather than management), and suddenly, a section of the factory becomes the focus for disruption. The other work groups in the factory will probably meet to decide how their own members should react to the issue, and the reaction is generally in support of the disgruntled group.

Neighborhood Organizations

In addition to the *xiaozu, neighborhood organizations*—first established in 1954—also tie individuals into a national system of social control. The major function of neighborhood organizations is the registration of households and individuals. No one can move into a neighborhood without being officially registered. Those who cannot be registered are not allowed to stay.

This practice was established to control migration from rural areas to the overcrowded cities. Neighborhood organizations maintain dossiers on all members and note their political reliability, cooperativeness, and general behavior. These files go from one neighborhood organization to another when a person changes residences.

Once registered, the individual must report any residential-related changes, such as visitors, relatives moving in, marriages, or births. A committee watches for unauthorized births and gives information on birth control and child care. Another committee settles minor family disputes, decides on minor legal infractions such as juvenile truancy, and investigates family violence and neglect. A husband who drinks too much may receive a visit of a delegation from this committee to "educate" him in proper behavior.

As important, scarce materials and rationed goods, such as cooking fuel and cloth for clothing, are allocated through neighborhood organizations. In the past, coal, grain, sugar, meats, fish, and even bicycles were also unobtainable without the proper authorization of neighborhood committees. Now, although such functions are no longer necessary, they remain in place in case they are needed in the future. Welfare pensions are often distributed through these bureaucracies, as are bonuses for limiting families to one child or for undergoing sterilization.

Many of China's larger cities offer families bonuses to match inflation or the cost of food. The municipal government of Tianjin, a city in north China, gives each official resident 17.5 yuan a month as a food allowance. This accounted for 27 percent of an average family's monthly income during 1989. These subsidies are distributed through the neighborhood organization networks.

Each neighborhood organization has full-time officials and office space. This space can be used for meetings, local libraries, educational programs, and similar activities as well as for organized sports and adult education. Some organizations maintain fire and police stations, day care centers, and emergency medical facilities.

These organizations are primarily agencies of social control as well as social welfare. Each area has observers who note everyone's movements, report on visitors, and keep track of all activities. Meetings are called whenever central government officials want to issue proclamations or educate members on a certain matter, such as changes in official policy. Neighborhood groups also provide members for parades and similar public spectacles.

The drive to reduce China's birth rate centers on neighborhood associations, though work-related *danwei* groups are also heavily involved in birth-related issues. Committees register each couple and check for unregistered births. Couples cannot have children unless the appropriate committee allows the births. A wife pregnant with a second child will endure numerous visits from committee members to discuss the possibility of abortion and for "family responsibility" sessions. Representatives make certain a pregnant woman attends prenatal medical checks if her pregnancy has been approved.

In summary, the private lives of urban Chinese are closely tied to neighborhood organizations. Foreign employers must make certain they do not demand of their workers behavior not approved by these organizations.

Endnotes

1. *Wall Street Journal,* 30 August 1989, A-11.
2. James McGregor, "Hainan Province, Once a Paradise for Capitalism in China, Is Now Lost," *Wall Street Journal,* 23 July 1991, A-13.
3. Coured Schirokauer, *A Brief History of Chinese and Japanese Civilizations* (New York: Harcourt Brace & Jovanovich, 1978).

For Further Reading

Browning, Gram. *If Everyone Bought One Shoe: American Capitalism in Communist China.* New York: Hill and Wang, 1989.

Chinese Population Information and Data Center. *Chinese Population Data Handbook.* Beijing: Chinese Population and Data Center, 1983.

Chu, Lynn. "Innocents Abroad: The Chimera of the Chinese Market." *Atlantic,* October 1990, 55-68.

Economist, The. *The Economist Book of Vital World Statistics.* New York: Times Books, 1990.

Hong, Ma. *Modern China Economic Facts.* Beijing: Chinese Academy of Social Sciences Press, 1982.

Organization Resources Counselors, Inc. *Multinationals in China: Human Resources Practices and Issues in the PRC.* New York: Rockefeller Center, 1986.

Overholt, William H. *The Rise of China: How Economic Reform Is Creating a New Superpower.* New York: Norton, 1993.

Schell, Orville. *To Get Rich Is Glorious: China in the 80s.* Revised and updated edition. New York: New American Library, 1986.

Smith, Christopher J. *China: People and Places in the Land of One Billion.* Boulder, Colorado: Westview Press, 1991.

Spence, Jonathan D. *The Search for Modern China.* New York: Norton, 1990.

Taihe, Huang. "Development of China's SEZ." *Beijing Review,* April 8-14, 1992, 20-26.

3

Problems and Prospects

Foreigners should be especially concerned with the unique risks of doing business with officials or private individuals in China. The possibilities of extremely large profits and markets often blind foreign investors to the dangers and limitations. In this chapter we will discuss some of the major problems faced by foreigners who wish to develop a presence in China.

In our discussion we present the most pessimistic scenarios, not to scare off potential investors but to prepare them for entering the Chinese market. It is much better to confront the problems of doing business in China as soon as possible. Delayed confrontation may allow unexpected issues to become major crises at a time when a foreign investor has less leverage.

In a survey of Americans who have investments in China, the US-China Business Council reported a number of agencies that were helpful in resolving investment-related problems. Careful preparation and help on the part of friendly agents can increase the chances of success.

Officials in locally based and national organizations and ministries are valuable resources in solving problems. Many Chinese officials (though not all) are eager to help foreign investors become successful, and it is usually to their advantage to help foreigners. However, officials are always more helpful in solving problems and crises when personal relationships have been established.

Right to Dismiss Workers

China's leaders are very concerned that economic development not destroy the social status quo by causing unemployment. Therefore, Chinese laws limit the rights of foreigners to fire workers without serious cause. It is often both difficult and time-consuming—if not impossible—to dismiss workers, especially after a worker's probationary period has been completed.

During the first three-quarters of 1993, Chinese officials estimated that 850,000 persons were unemployed. There are also between 50 and 100 million migrants (floating workers), many without housing. The government wishes to reduce unemployment to below 3 percent. However, the rural areas can no longer absorb excess labor, as they did during the mid-1980s. Consequently, officials do not wish to give foreigners the right to dismiss workers who would otherwise have no other means of support except government-sponsored welfare. Final contracts should always include clauses giving investors leeway to dismiss workers. For example, a clause might specify that management can dismiss workers who habitually operate machinery inappropriately.

Lack of Maintenance and Infrastructure

The lack of concern for maintenance on the part of many Chinese workers is a major difficulty. Therefore, investors should pay careful attention to future costs of maintenance and repair. Few budgets and cost projections presented by the Chinese will include line items for maintenance and repairs or for spare parts. Foreigners negotiating a joint venture or a presence in China should be concerned with these hidden and often unanticipated costs, including costs for training workers to handle and maintain their machines and equipment.

As any foreigner who has stayed in Chinese-managed hotels or office buildings can testify, building maintenance is often ignored in China. Leaks, chipped paint, and other signs of deterioration are frequently evident. The same neglect occurs in manufacturing situations. Machines, for example, are given little maintenance and preventive care. Nor do Chinese workers often concern themselves with the correct operation of machines. Automobiles, also, receive little maintenance and care and frequently are driven until they completely break down. In the past, Chinese organizations found it easier to order new automobiles than to obtain spare parts or train mechanics.

Because repair and parts replacement costs will probably be higher in China than elsewhere, we strongly advise foreign investors to include repair and maintenance clauses in proposals and contracts. Such issues will be ignored if they are not specifically dealt with during contractual negotiations. Negotiations should also include provisions for costs of training workers to run and maintain equipment. Chinese officials often offer special tax advantages to offset training costs, though they may not volunteer this information. In addition, negotiations should specify ways the Chinese government and Chinese partners, if any, can reduce the investor's maintenance and training costs.

Maintenance of Work Areas

Another maintenance-related issue is the relative lack of interest Chinese workers have in keeping work areas clean and materials-free. Chinese workers are very tolerant of trash, and most do not accept responsibility for keeping their work areas clean, especially when the mess is caused by others. Accumulated trash can threaten safety, as when oily cloths are allowed to pile up in a corner or when discarded material is left on the ground to trip pedestrians or block moving equipment.

Workers are likely to feel that housekeeping issues are their prerogative and that they have the right to decide how neat and clean (or not) individual work areas should be. This attitude, which is very hard to change, is generally unanticipated by foreign investors. Maintenance and housekeeping issues should be carefully discussed during contractual negotiations.

One possible solution to housekeeping and maintenance problems is to reward workers when they meet certain goals, such as keeping a work area clean and grease-free or leaving no material about when a team ends a shift. It is certain that members of the next shift will not feel obligated to clean up after the previous shift. Rewarding workers for housekeeping and maintenance is one way to convince them that management takes these issue very seriously. Another solution is to develop a bonus system.

Infrastructure Weaknesses

China lacks an infrastructure capable of supporting its present economy or of meeting additional more modern demands. Many resources taken for granted in other countries simply do not exist in China. International telecommunication resources in the larger cities are generally adequate, especially in the hotels catering to international customers. However, internal telephone resources are strained to the limit, and it is often impossible to get a line for hours. When a local line is finally obtained, the connection may produce too much static for reliable communication. This is one reason cellular phones are a status symbol and are in great demand in China.

In addition, energy supplies are severely overloaded. Local officials may promise potential investors a certain amount of energy— say, coal or electricity sufficient to maintain a five-day production schedule for five years—but will probably not be able to keep such promises. Brownouts are common throughout China, and despite official promises, there is no guarantee of constant surge-free electricity. Whether China's electrical resources can keep up with future demands is questionable. A second nuclear power plant has recently opened at Daya Bay in Guangdong province near Hong Kong, and another plant is due to be commissioned soon.

China also became a net importer of oil in 1994 for the first time in decades. Recently, several large oil reserves have been discovered, and development has been leased to a number of foreign consortiums. But development and the delivery of oil products to consumers will demand time and huge investments.

Other elements of the infrastructure are often inadequate. Highways are few and repair spotty, so transportation problems exist that are seldom found in more industrialized nations. Many localities are unwilling to repair roads that are used by outsiders passing through from one province to another. Roads and rail lines often lack linkage, so that it is difficult to travel long distances in a direct manner. At times, provincial and municipal officials erect roadblocks in order to demand "fees" for passing through a region.

The availability of adequate water supplies for industrial and human uses remains a major problem. Most drinking water is polluted and must be boiled before being drunk or used in cooking.

Historically, Chinese government officials have been concerned with developing adequate water supplies for agricultural purposes. Rice farming demands large amounts of water during specified periods, so reliable water supplies are mandatory. These resources are already strained, and many cannot be diverted to the industrial sector. Investments demanding steady, large amounts of water, such as breweries and steel mills, should be carefully analyzed.

The educational system also presents unique problems. The Cultural Revolution closed schools for almost a decade, so that Chinese in their mid-thirties to mid-forties often are relatively ill-educated. Further, the Chinese system of education stresses rote memorization and theory. Many well-educated Chinese are not prepared to be creative or to think independently.

Although Chinese scientists are well prepared in basic science and in theory, they are seldom educated in how to deal with practical problems. As a result, there are many Chinese scientists/theorists but few well-trained engineers. Nor are Chinese scientists prepared to use their knowledge to design products or to innovate. Foreigners should expect to provide much more in-house training than is customary.

Since China does not yet have a consumer-oriented society, many office and factory supplies—from fax paper to paper clips to batteries for laptop PCs—are not readily available. Also, the quality of Chinese business products is so low that they are usually unusable. Consequently, foreigners must expect to plan in much greater detail and to import many items that are commonplace in the United States and elsewhere.

Government Intervention

Another risk experienced by foreign investors is unanticipated, rapid, government reversal of policy and unilateral intervention. Beijing and local officials are quite willing to add taxes and fees without warning. Officials may also unilaterally change contractual agreements, even after a contract and proposal have been approved.

The Chinese view of the nature of contracts—that it is possible to change contractual agreements when the original conditions no longer apply—is based on two assumptions: (1) current economic policies are understood as being experimental; the Chinese are introducing new economic procedures, such as selected forms of capitalism, to learn which ones encourage economic growth without causing undesirable social and political changes; (2) many economic reforms are local and apply only to specific areas such as the Shanghai municipality or Guangzhou. Policies deemed successful will be kept and perhaps introduced elsewhere. Reforms considered counterproductive will be ended, no matter the inconvenience to foreign investors.

A recent example of such changes in policy is the experience of the Continental Can Company. Continental Can was welcomed in China during the late 1980s. The company's major motivation for entering the China market was the demand for canned drinks—the demand for cans and pop-top tabs at that time was greater than the available supply. Unfortunately, the depressed economy, inflation, and the drop in tourism after the 1989 Tiananmen Square tragedy reduced the demand for canned drinks. These were unpredictable events that could have happened in many other parts of the world. In 1990, however, Beijing officials also decided that canned beverages were a wasteful use of scarce resources, and canned drinks were banned from all state functions and banquets. This additionally reduced the demand for Continental Can's products, creating a large surplus of cans.

Because of the depressed economic conditions and lack of foreign currency, Beijing officials doubled the tariffs on imported aluminum materials at that time and declared a new tax on canned-drink consumption. Thus—almost overnight—Chinese officials became anti-canned drink and began to use their considerable administrative power to decrease can-related imports and consumption. These changes were made without warning or consultation with Continental Can officials.

Contracts are also seen by Chinese as flexible if the conditions existing when a contract was signed have changed. Recently, the Construction Bank of China approved a massive US$3.3 billion project to construct a Beijing-Hong Kong railway, involving 300,000 workers and the construction of over five hundred bridges. This railway will make available to foreign investors large areas of—as yet—undeveloped Chinese resources. China's leaders also wish to decentralize the location of foreign investments, which now are primarily in coastal regions—near Hong Kong and across from Taiwan. With government support, the new railway will allow easier access to areas where land and labor are much cheaper. Wages in isolated areas can be as much as one-tenth of those in Shanghai and the coastal areas.

However, government officials could decide to cancel this project, even after a number of foreign investments have been established on the basis of the expanded transportation system. Should the political climate with Hong Kong change, officials could stop construction in order to isolate Hong Kong. Officials could also decide to limit the expansion of locations for capitalist development due to fears of social and political unrest.

A likelier scenario is the cancellation of the Beijing-Hong Kong project in reaction to the current high rate of inflation (more than 20 percent) in China or in order to allocate the funds to another project. When such changes occur, foreign investors can ask for a review or for mediation, but in China the risk of government unilateral action always exists.

Entry Requirements

Because China remains a partially closed nation, a visa is required for tourist and business purposes. A valid passport is also required. When applying for a business visa, one must present to the Chinese visa officials a copy of an invitation letter from a Chinese government office or from a Chinese business concern. Essentially, foreigners must be invited by an organization before they can enter China. The Chinese host also must submit a copy of the formal invitation to the visa office.

The invitation notes the general purpose of the visit. It also contains the passport number, expected duration of stay, and number in the party. Extensions are easily given but are time-consuming to obtain. The Chinese host must ask for a visa extension from local security officials.

Finding A Chinese Partner

We recommend entering the Chinese market by developing a joint venture with a Chinese partner rather than as an independent investor. The Chinese market is too unfamiliar to Westerners, and a Chinese partner can provide cultural as well as other insights. When beginning a new venture in China this can be accomplished by hiring host nationals. An easier way of entry is to invest in a state-owned company (usually one in financial trouble) that the government wishes to privatize.

As an example, during 1993 the Hunan Province leaders auctioned a number of state-owned enterprises in order to form joint ventures with foreign investors. Hunan Province is relatively backward in terms of development and will remain isolated until completion of the Beijing-Guandong railway. The province lacks adequate electric supplies, and its railroad resources are overtaxed. But mining and agricultural resources are ample, and workers at Changsha, the Hunan capital, earn 300 yuan per month, compared with at least 500 yuan on the coast. Land costs 20 yuan per square foot in Changsha compared to over 100 yuan per square foot in coastal Shenzhen. Someone wishing to establish a joint venture in Hunan will be encouraged to do so by Hunan officials and leaders.[1]

Joint Ventures

Joint-venture buy-outs are usually welcomed by workers, since employees of foreign firms generally receive three to four or more times the average salaries of those employed in government-owned enterprises. By contrast, government-employed workers enjoy higher fringe benefits, including such items as day care, subsidized housing, free or partially subsidized medical care, retirement benefits, a much slower work pace, and total job security. The payoff exchange is that while joint-venture employees lose very ample fringe benefits and total job security (called the "iron rice bowl"), they earn much more and can better take part in China's emerging consumer society.

An example of the attraction of working in a foreign joint venture is described by N. Zhang, in the account of Mr. Wu, a college-educated Chinese in his twenties.[2] His first job was with the Chinese park service, with a salary of 200 yuan (US$35) per month plus bonuses. He also received free health care. He joined a foreign investment firm as a trainee earning 600 yuan per month with an increase to 900 yuan per month after a three-month training period. For a greatly increased salary, he works longer hours and has much less job security.

Entrepreneurs, if they complete a successful deal, may earn at one stroke what a government worker could earn in a lifetime. These are the instant millionaires who receive great publicity. Most Chinese, however, would choose a middle course between being an unprotected entrepreneur and a worker in a state-owned enterprise—that of the joint venture. (Note: The term *government worker* is usually interchangeable with "worker in a state-owned firm." We use the term *official* to denote a person who is part of the government bureaucracy.)

Joint ventures often ease certain potential problems, such as leasing land or buildings, since government officials do not want to sell commercial land to foreigners. The Chinese government is much more likely to encourage joint ventures than to promote other forms of investments, though foreigners have been given much leeway in how they wish to establish a presence in China. For foreigners who are unfamiliar with the Chinese business environment or who have few local contacts, the establishment of a joint venture remains the best way to enter China.

Joint ventures can take advantage of numerous development policies established by government and local officials. Incomes in coastal boom towns in the Special Economic Zones are six to eight times higher than average incomes in the more isolated inland provinces. Even within a province such as Guandong, cash incomes (excluding benefits such as subsidized medicine) vary between areas on the coast and those in the mountains. A policy adopted in 1993 provides for the linkage of a poor area to a wealthy city such as Guangzhou. Larger ventures that can invest both in a boom city and in a poor area receive tax and other advantages from officials.

There are four general types of joint ventures: the *equity* joint venture, the *contractual* joint venture, the *wholly foreign-owned* venture and the *compensation trade* venture. Foreign investment in China has been primarily of the first two types.

Equity Joint Ventures

The *equity joint venture* (EJV) is a limited liability corporation jointly invested in and operated by Chinese and foreign partners. The Chinese government prefers and encourages this type of investment. Profits are distributed either according to the proportion of investment contributed by each partner or as stated in the contractual agreements. The minimum share of investment by the foreign partner must be at least 25 percent. In practice, the foreign party usually is responsible for between 40 and 60 percent of the venture's equity.

EJVs have a "legal person" status and are therefore protected under Chinese law. A joint venture remains under the guidance of the state, although the degree of guidance will vary. Equity joint ventures are assessed at an income tax rate of 30 percent. A local tax of 1 percent is common, making the effective income tax rate 33 percent. Tax rate reductions are available, depending on type of enterprise and other circumstances.

According to the US-China Business Council, EJVs offer a number of advantages over other forms of investment:

- Laws regulating EJVs are relatively well developed.
- EJVs are allowed to sell on the domestic market.
- EJVs may receive raw materials at subsidized prices.

A major disadvantage of EJVs is that termination procedures have not yet been clearly established, so foreign partners may find it expensive if they wish to cancel an EJV agreement.

Contractual Joint Ventures

Contractual joint ventures (CJVs), often called *cooperative management,* allow for more flexibility and negotiation freedom. Assets and liabilities may be kept separately by the partners, may be merged in various proportions, or may be used to develop another venture. The income tax rates for CJVs are the same as for the EJVs. When each partner operates independently of the other, however, the foreign party may be taxed at rates up to 50 percent.

An advantage of CJVs is that profit-sharing agreements are flexible; the foreign partner can receive a proportionally larger share of the earnings at the start of the venture and less in the future. Since the type of state-owned enterprise most likely to be sold to foreigners is one that is failing to earn a profit, it may take a number of years to achieve profitability. Distribution of earnings is a flexible matter to be discussed during negotiations.

The greatest advantage of the CJV structure is that Chinese law allows it the greatest amount of flexibility in management, sharing profits, and financial investments. No minimum investment is required, so smaller enterprises can establish their own ventures appropriate to their individual assets or can combine with other foreign firms to pool assets.

Another advantage of CJVs is that the agreement can be more easily dissolved than can other types of ventures. A foreign investor may not be able to end an agreement quickly if it is unprofitable, or if the local partner is turns out to be completely inappropriate. Since contractual joint ventures are defined as temporary in nature, losses can be more easily limited.

This advantage is offset by the fact that taxes are higher for contractual joint ventures than for other ventures. Another disadvantage of the contractual joint venture is that it usually has a fixed time limit before it is dissolved, and negotiations determine the length of the venture. *At the termination of the contract, the joint venture and all of its assets are turned over to the Chinese partner.* In addition, the legal framework for CJVs remains undeveloped. The legal protection of CJVs is unclear at this time.

Wholly Foreign-owned Enterprise

The third type of foreign investment structure is the *wholly foreign-owned enterprise* (WFOE). In this case, the foreign investors receive all the profits, bear all the risks, and are the sole investors. The income tax rates vary from 30 to 50 percent, though deductions are available. The foreign investor must lease land and utilities from appropriate government agencies and must deal with the local employment office to obtain labor.

Because WFOEs are relatively new to China, the legal system has not yet been fully developed to deal with them. Negotiations must be complete and highly detailed, though there is little guarantee that the legal system will protect the rights of the foreign investor. WFOEs generally export most of their production rather than produce products for Chinese consumer markets.

Business conditions are so different in China that foreign investors must be highly skilled to achieve success without a Chinese partner. The investors should be experienced China hands with a full command of Mandarin and an understanding of Chinese business and government affairs. American owners and managers of WFOEs in China are generally ethnic Chinese, though there are exceptions.

The WFOEs form a small minority of foreign investments in China. Digital Equipment Corporation, for example, manufactures computer components for export. Flextronics Inc. also produces computer components, primarily printed circuit boards, for export. CP China Company manufactures compressors for export. (A list of American companies currently doing business in China is available from the US-China Business Council.)

Compensation Trade Agreements

A fourth possible foreign investment strategy is the *compensation trade agreement*. Essentially, the foreign investor exchanges technology, training, and foreign currency credit (if necessary) in exchange for goods produced by loaned equipment. The products are the compensation for the foreign investment.

Other agreements are possible, but they demand extensive knowledge of local conditions, and familiarity with Chinese culture. William H. Overholt illustrates the possible flexibility available to those who are familiar with how business is done in China. Overholt asked an ethnic Chinese banker in Hong Kong why Westerners, and Americans in particular, have experienced a higher rate of investment failure as compared to Hong Kong investors who are ethnic Chinese. The banker's response was that

the Americans try to do everything by the book. They show up in town and immediately go to the mayor's office and ask what the rules are. He tells them the rules, and they spend months sorting out all the official details. He assigns them a factory site and they start building. As soon as they start, a pile of bricks shows up in the middle of the road. If they move the bricks, the local people sue them for breaking their bricks. When they finally get rid of the bricks, a herd of goats shows up in the road. They're always in trouble. There's always something new blocking the road or a new government regulation they never heard of before. We do it differently. We go into town and look around for a good site. When we find what we want, we call the local people together and ask them if they'd like a new factory that pays much better wages. They always do. After this, we ask them what they want. They always want a school and a clinic and sometimes a few other things. So we build these for them; such things are very cheap in China. Then we go down to the mayor's office with a delegation of local people and they tell him what we're going to do. He wouldn't dare stand in their way.[3]

Foreign investors can now establish direct contact with Chinese companies without using a government office as intermediary. For those with limited knowledge of Chinese companies and their resources, letters of inquiry can be sent to local Chinese government offices or to the Ministry of Foreign Economic Relations and Trade. (See "Helpful Addresses" at the end of this chapter.) A summary of basic documents required for joint ventures is listed in Exhibit 3-1.

Potential investors may also contact Chinese embassies and consulates in the United States. Each has a Commercial Office to help foreigners locate possible joint-venture partners and investment possibilities. Another source of contact is the China International Trust and Investment Corporation (CITIC), where initial ideas and proposals may be sent. This commission is the highest authority in China involving foreign investments, and ultimately accepts or rejects any projects involving foreigners and foreign currency, or most matters involving economic development. CITIC sends numerous missions abroad in order to promote its favored projects.

Other Chinese government and municipal offices have as much or almost as much responsibility. The four most important commis-

---

Exhibit 3-1. Summary of Basic Documents

Joint Feasibility Study

A report that describes the general features of the proposed venture. The benefits and costs of the venture are presented, especially the benefits to China and the area. This includes mention of the financing the foreign partner expects to make, such as foreign credit investments, importation of latest technology, training of workers, etc. There should be mention of energy and local materials needed. This document is formally presented to the State Planning Commission and municipal authorities.

Technology Transfer Contract

A report containing the technological requirements of the venture, how imported machinery and parts will be financed, and so forth. The amount of training, in the United States or in China, of Chinese personnel is specified in this report. Pollution and environmental concerns are also addressed.

Joint Venture Contract

This is the actual contract negotiated by all concerned parties, including the government. It should be as detailed and complete as possible, and nothing should be assumed because cultural differences can cause unanticipated conflicts.

Source: William H. Newman, *Birth of a Successful Joint Venture* (Lanham, Maryland: University Press of America, 1992), 63.

---

sions are located in Beijing, Shanghai, and Guangdong. In the United States, a useful source of information for would-be investors is the US-China Business Council.

Addresses and telephone numbers for the CITIC, the four major China commissions, and the US-China Business Council are also listed at the end of this chapter.

Submitting a Proposal

Having located a potential joint-venture partner, a "written proposal of cooperation" must be sent to the Chinese party. The proposal is essentially a declaration of intent and outlines the major features of the business relationship. The proposal states the goals of the venture (the manufacture of goods to be exported or distributed and sold in China) and the form the relationship will take (joint venture, leasing of resources, compensation trade, wholly or partially owned enterprise). The written proposal also includes division of profits, percentage of investment for each party, extent and source of funding.

The proposal is forwarded by the Chinese contact to the appropriate government and municipal officials, who will judge whether it meets the criteria for foreign investors and for the economic development of the Chinese nation. The proposal is also evaluated to determine whether the Chinese partner can meet its side of the agreement and whether outside funding by various municipal and government agencies is necessary—to build access roads or to provide additional energy to meet the requirements of the venture, for example.

Should the proposal be endorsed by the proper officials, it then becomes the framework for face-to-face negotiations. The proposal, in its final form, should be as detailed as possible in defining the responsibilities and aims of each party. While the proposal at this stage does not entail any legal responsibilities, it forms the basis for further negotiation. It may be difficult to change the basic outline of the proposal in the future.

Establishing Negotiations

The Chinese party then invites the foreign party to China to begin negotiations. In the past, foreign negotiators were forced to negotiate only in China. Negotiations increasingly are taking place outside mainland China. The foreign party, however, may be expected to finance the visit of the potential venture partners. Many Chinese businesspersons may not have the foreign credits available to travel abroad. Nevertheless, it is much more common (and prudent) for the foreign party to send inspection teams, and then negotiators, to the planned venture location.

If negotiations progress satisfactorily, a *joint feasibility study* report is submitted by both parties to the appropriate national, regional, or municipal authorities. (A feasibility study includes the major features of the proposed project, such as division of profits, total investment, what each partner—if any—will contribute in terms of finances, and methods of marketing.) After examination by government officials, it may be necessary to carry out field studies, test technology, measure quality levels, and so forth and submit a more detailed second feasibility study.

Once the feasibility study is accepted by officials, the two parties can begin the legal and formal phases of negotiations. Usually, the Chinese partners will invite the foreign party to begin negotiations in China. The foreign party can also invite Chinese representatives to visit, but the customary option is for the foreigners to go to China, at least during the initial negotiating stages. If Chinese are invited to the United States or to foreign company offices located outside of China—in Hong Kong, for example—it is proper to pay the major expenses of the visiting team.

A contract with legal standing can now be negotiated and drawn up. Until this point, however, lawyers and legal advisers play a minor and very informal part of the negotiations. Now, "articles of association" can be developed, according to current Chinese law, and presented to appropriate officials for acceptance. When approval of the formal contract is given, the new venture partners apply for registration with the local agency responsible for foreign investors.

China's development is dynamic, and major changes have been introduced every few years as Chinese officials become more familiar with foreigners and with global trade. A proposal may be unattractive to Chinese officials at one time but be highly acceptable later. It is important to remain flexible and able to respond to rapid changes in policy.

In spite of this need to adapt to changing conditions, it is also necessary to be very careful during the preliminary stages, to plan for all eventualities, and to prepare for issues not considered problematical in other countries.

Tax Incentives for Foreign Investors

Chinese officials have drastically altered China's tax systems to encourage foreign investment. The tax system now favors export-oriented investments or those that introduce state-of-the-art technology. However, China's tax system affecting foreigners is less than two decades old and continues to change.

Like other parts of economic reform, the tax system often offers unique conditions based on the nature of a project, how important the project is to officials, or specific circumstances. There is, in essence, little national-level standardization of tax codes or their application. Projects that bring in more foreign currency, for example, may be taxed less than are projects that involve less foreign credits.

Taxation is also highly variable by location. A foreign-owned enterprise income tax rate is halved if the intended location is in the Special Economic Zones of Shenzhen, Zhuhai, Shantou, or Xiamen, areas that Beijing officials want developed. Manufacturing enterprises may also receive tax advantages over service firms.

Another variable in taxation is the time factor. Enterprises that contract for a minimum ten-year investment receive two-year tax holidays, starting the first year profits are made, and a 50 percent reduction in taxes for the next three years. Additionally, export-oriented enterprises receive tax deductions if they export 70 percent or more of their products. Enterprises that import large amounts of technologically advanced machinery and spare parts also receive tax exemptions, based on how much of their manufacturing facilities and support (trucks, telecommunications, and so forth) are imported. From the foregoing examples, it is clear that China's tax officials are highly pragmatic: taxes are central tools to encourage economic development in the directions desired by China's leaders.

Foreign investors can negotiate with Chinese tax officials for special tax rates, tax holidays, and exemptions of various types. In essence, tax officials are willing to tailor a unique tax system to encourage desired investors.

The basic corporate tax rate is 33 percent of income (called the Unified Tax). There is also a Consolidated Tax for industrial and commercial enterprises. The Consolidated Tax is levied at various stages of the production process, including the importation of material into China.

Unified Tax

The *Unified Tax,* as discussed earlier, allows for a number of exemptions. There are various tax holidays and reductions of rates for newly established enterprises. The tax rate is also reduced for low-profit enterprises. Enterprises that locate in underdeveloped or remote areas can be given tax reductions for ten years after the first exemptions expire. Exporters who export more than 70 percent of their products made in China also are given reduced tax rates, though a minimum income tax of 10 percent is mandated by law. Investors who reinvest their profits for at least five years receive a full refund for all reinvestments.

Consolidated Tax

Reduction of taxes imposed for the importation of supplies and machinery is usually available. These imports must be machinery or other goods (spare parts or similar items) that cannot be obtained in China. Generally, such materials have to be purchased by the foreign partner at its own cost. Low-profit enterprises may apply for temporary tax reductions because of difficulties in meeting minimum tax payments. These changes are negotiated on a case-by-case basis.

It is possible for officials to impose additional taxes and fees at a moment's notice. For example, if electrical power is in short supply, a municipality might add a surcharge for electricity. Such levies can also be negotiated. Tax officials can also demand revenues on goods that have been produced but not yet sold. In 1989, Shanghai Johnson, Ltd., which is 60-percent-owned by U.S.-based S.C. Johnson & Sons, had an agreement to sell shampoo and shoe polish products to government-owned distribution monopolies. When the Chinese economy slowed during that year, government-owned enterprises became cash-starved and cut down drastically on orders. The result of this economic downturn was that Shanghai Johnson could not dispose of or receive payment for a large stockpile of goods. But tax officials insisted that all production be taxed, and the company suddenly owed the government US$1 million during a period of greatly reduced sales.

Property Ownership and Taxes

Property taxation is a new phenomenon in China, and the tax system is still developing. Rural land is mostly collectively or individually owned. Urban land, however, is owned by the government, as has been previously noted, and Chinese officials are reluctant to sell land to foreigners. Most land used by foreigners is "owned" by the Chinese partner or is leased to the venture by the government. Regional and municipal governments have tried to develop a land use tax that does not imply permanent control (private ownership) by the taxpayer.

In Communist ideology, land is a gift of nature and has no value in an economic sense. Land, like air or water, is a common resource to be enjoyed by all. As a result, the concept of private ownership of land is relatively undeveloped.

The legal system also has little say as yet concerning the rights of ownership. Lacking a free real estate market on which to base a tax rate, it is difficult if not impossible to evaluate the fairness of a land-use tax. Nor is it possible yet to project land prices and associated tax rates.

Since much land is owned by the government and allotted by officials to various parties, land use is haphazard. Consequently, there has been little concern for zoning or for assigning land according to economic standards. Unlike land use in the West, where the cost of land has imposed some order on business location, Chinese use of land has not been based on economics. In Liaoning Province, for example, over 80 percent of the province's more than five thousand factories are located within cities.

Foreign investors should be careful in selecting a site and in negotiating rights of ownership. The Chinese constitution was amended in 1988 to include the clause "the right of land use can be transferred in accordance with the law." But since the legal system is still evolving, it is impossible to predict whether a foreign investor can buy outright tracts of land or what other rights will be included. No one knows today whether it will be possible to sell or sublease land easily. Also, although there is as yet no official real estate market, a black market in urban land exists.

In urban areas, a foreign investor may lease a plot of land allocated to a Chinese firm. The payment may be in cash or through barter. For example, a firm may lease a plot of land from a local enterprise in payment of part of the firm's future production or in exchange for an agreement to build apartment housing, with half of the apartments going to the original "owners." Land-lease agreements need to be highly creative in China.

In the Shenzhen Special Economic Zone, developers were allowed to lease land through an open auction sponsored by the local government. Other areas and municipalities are also experimenting with various land-buying or leasing strategies. However, the rights of lessors or owners remain unclear.

Another problem faced by foreign investors is the inability to predict land-use costs. It is possible that leasing agreements will be changed as the value of land increases and officials try to increase tax revenues. Leasing agreements should be carefully negotiated and assumed to be temporary.

Types of Corruption

A major problem with doing business in China is the constant need to deal with various types of corruption. Arne J. de Keijzer, an experienced consultant, estimates that up to one-half of all contracts dealing with Chinese include some type of corruption.[4] Often, government officials are not prone to act on a request unless certain "favors" have been offered. At times, government officials demand favors in order to issue required certificates.

Those involved in long-range projects in China are less likely to be faced with demands for extra gifts and payments than are those who wish to complete a one-time deal quickly. For such investors, officials are likely to declare that new fees or taxes need to be paid immediately. Such demands can be appealed and avoided, but doing so takes time and knowledge of the local bureaucracy.

An extreme example of official corruption and how it affected a foreign investor who established an engineering plant in Shenzhen was reported by Brewer S. Stone.[5] The investor was told that five approvals were needed to begin operations, and he paid bribes to each official to speed the process. He was then told that an additional ten official permissions were needed to continue. The bribes eventually became larger than the total cost of his investment, including land and needed capital.

A favorite solicitation is a subsidized trip abroad under the guise of an inspection tour. Another popular demand is for the foreign partner to sponsor a child's education abroad. A third common demand is the hiring of relatives, whether they work or not. Many foreign joint-venture partners find that their Chinese counterpart has hired an excess number of workers that are supported by the foreign investment. Avoiding this surplus cost necessitates tight control of hiring procedures by the foreign partner and must be discussed during precontractual negotiations.

It is difficult to avoid most forms of legal and extralegal extortion. Foreigners are routinely charged more for services and goods, such as hotel rooms, railway tickets, and airplane reservations. Such solicitation is an extension of the feeling that all foreigners are wealthy and should pay more for the privilege of being in China.

Motivating Workers

While labor laws and a more detailed description of China's workers and their attitudes are found in a later chapter, we wish to warn potential investors of the difficulty of motivating Chinese workers. Chinese entrepreneurs are hard-working and self-starters, but the average Chinese employee lacks the desire to work hard or to accept responsibility to become a better, more productive, worker. This condition results from almost fifty years of Communist rule, during which workers were protected from competition and when workers who did not act like all the others were soon punished. In addition, the "iron rice bowl" system of complete job security irrespective of work accomplished has discouraged workers and managers from increasing productivity. The Chinese government has recognized this major problem of motivation and has attempted some reforms. But these attempts are still in their infancy, and the Chinese labor force remains one of the most inefficient in the world.

Consequently, foreign investors need to develop innovative reward systems to motivate workers. One such scheme that can be adapted to local needs is the Chinese government's 100 Points Bonus System (see Exhibit 3-2).[6] This bonus system rewards workers when they, or their teams, fulfill pre-established goals. More important goals carry more points (bonuses), and bonuses are awarded according to the number of bonus points a worker accumulates. Workers gain bonuses when they have achieved 100 or more points. An advantage of this plan is its flexibility, since different targets or goals are weighted according to their importance. The relative weights change as conditions also change. In addition, targets can be added or deleted, and the number of points needed to receive bonuses can be altered, according to changing needs.

At the start of a project, housekeeping problems are probably a major issue. Building scraps and leftover materials need to be picked

Exhibit 3-2. 100 Points Bonus System

Target	Points
1. Output quantity	20
2. Quality	30
3. Cost	10
4. Safety	10
5. Productivity	10
6. Attendance	10
7. Profits	10
8. Equipment maintenance	10
9. Clean work area	10

Source: Sukhan Jackson, *Chinese Enterprise Management Reforms in Economic Perspective* (Berlin, Germany: Walter de Gruyter, 1992), 278.

up and discarded, and more bonus points should be offered for general trash pick up. Later, this target can be deemphasized and more encouragement given to maintenance, attendance, or other problems.

Investing in China

We have mentioned a number of times that investing in China, or dealing with Chinese for business-related purposes in general, demands great patience and special knowledge. Exhibit 3-3 lists some of the positive and negative aspects of investing in China. Since the Chinese opened their borders to foreign investment in 1979, progress has been uneven. The US-China Business Council has summarized some of the major problems faced by foreign investors by asking Americans what would they do differently if they could start over:

- Pay more attention to central authorities
- Take tougher stance during negotiations
- Locate on the coast
- Make sure local governments understand the project
- Plan bigger
- Educate own management better
- Locate near major raw materials source
- Prepare more detailed plans

Exhibit 3-3. Investing in China—Positives and Negatives

Positive Elements:	*Negative Elements:*
Largest domestic market in the world	Infrastructure strained and inadequate for development
Rich resources	Resources untapped
Large savings pool	High rates of inflation
Government focused on growth	Lack of a stable legal system
Large labor pool	Lack of work motivation and managerial skills
Growing consumer market	Uneven consumer prosperity
Welcomes foreign investors	Unilateral intervention by government officials

---

China's Consumer Market

A major positive factor in investing in China is China's large consumer market. In the past, China's population was too poor to buy much more than necessities. However, in recent years incomes have doubled, tripled, or more in certain areas, and Chinese families are beginning to take part in a greatly expanding consumer market. China's leaders have recognized this fact by opening consumer markets to foreign investors, something they forbade or discouraged ten years or so ago. While investors who wish to export goods out of China are still encouraged, those who wish to sell within China are also welcome, especially if the goods are produced in China.

China's Changing Consumers

China is poised at the start of a major consumer revolution. In 1991, only a minority of the Chinese owned sewing machines (13%), bicycles (36%), washing machines (9%), and televisions (18%). Although Chinese consumers remain extremely poor in comparison with those in other countries (see Exhibit 3-4), China's consumer markets have two general advantages: (1) the market includes over a billion potential buyers, and (2) the economy is growing at a high rate.

As of 1992, China had four million persons with an annual income of at least US$5,357. Sixteen million are defined as well-to-do, with a 1992 income of US$1,300-$1,700.[7] Since housing, medical, and other consumer expenses are heavily subsidized in China, consumer wealth should be increased by at least 30 percent when comparing it with other national incomes.

Exhibit 3-4. Per Capita Personal Consumption in Selected Asian Countries (In US$)

Japan	$15,341	Bangkok	$3,947
Taiwan	4,636	India	234
S. Korea	3,433	China	149
Malaysia	1,442	Urban areas	301
Thailand	998	Guangdong province	431

Source: Yoko Okumura, "The Consumer Market and Consumer Trends in China," *JETRO China Newsletter,* Nov.-Dec. 1993, 16.

Exhibit 3-5. U.S. Products in High Demand in China

Dental equipment	Packaging equipment
Textile machinery	Medicine and antibiotics
Telecommunication equipment, including cellular phones	Mining equipment
	Baby care items
Oil/gas exploration equipment	Health foods
Fast food establishments	Engineering services
Machinery	Chemical raw materials
Agri-chemicals	Plastics
Motorcycles	Timber
Tobacco	Cotton
Fertilizer	Aircraft
Paper	Wheat
Fertilizer	Scientific equipment

While per capita cash wealth is low compared to that of Western countries, China's population is experiencing a consumer demand that local firms cannot meet (see Exhibit 3-5). From 1978 to 1990, the average salaried income increased almost fourfold. During the same period, the sales of consumer goods increased fivefold. Just as China's leaders have encouraged investment in the technological and export sectors, they are beginning to encourage foreign investors who wish to produce consumer goods for domestic consumption.

Endnotes

1. Kathy Chen, "China's Hunan Province Hopes to Match Neighbors," *Asian Wall Street Journal* (weekly), 14 June 1993, 1,18.
2. N. Zhang, "China's New Wave Makes for Difficult Choices," *Asian Wall Street Journal,* 5 April 1993, 16.
3. William H. Overholt, *The Rise of China: How Economic Reform Is Creating a Superpower* (New York: Norton, 1993).
4. Arne de Keijzer, *China: Business Strategies for the '90s* (Berkeley, California: Pacific View Press, 1992).
5. Brewer S. Stone, "Beating China's Rapacious Profiteers," *Wall Street Journal,* 4 October 1993, A12.

6. Sukhan Jackson, *Chinese Enterprise Management Reforms in Economic Perspective* (Berlin: Walter de Gruyter, 1992).
7. Yoko Okumura, "The Consumer Market and Consumer Trends in China," *JETRO China Newsletter*, Nov.-Dec. 1993, 16.

For Further Reading

Adi, Ignatius. "Foreign Ventures Feeling the Pinch of China Austerity." *Asian Wall Street Journal* (weekly), 18 December 1989, 1, 20.

Gu, Xiancheng, chief editor (1985). *The China Investing Guide*. London: Longman, 1986.

Newman, William H. *Birth of a Successful Joint Venture*. Lanham, Maryland: University Press of America, 1992.

Patrick, Andrew. "Tax Incentives in China." *Australian Accountant* (October 1993): 20-21.

The US-China Business Council. *Special Report on U.S. Investment in China*. New York: China Business Forum, 1990.

Helpful Addresses

The following organizations offer valuable help for those wishing to initiate contact with potential Chinese partners:

Beijing International Trust and Investment Corporation
1 Chong Wenmenwai Dongdadi, Beijing
Telephone: 753680 755885
Telex: 223337 BITIC CN
Cable: BITI BJ

CITIC
Two World Trade Center
Suite 2250
New York, NY 10048
Telephone: 212 938-0416
Telex: 229281 CITIC UR

Guangdong International Trust and Investment Corporation
4 Qiaoguang Road, Guangzhou, Guangdong
Telephone: 30975 35341
Telex: 44422 GITIC CN
Cable: 0975 GUANGZHOU

Ministry of Foreign Trade & Economic Cooperation (MOFTEC)
2 Dongchangan Jie Qu
Beijing 100731
Telephone: 1 5198114
Fax: 1 5129568

Shanghai Investment and Trust Corporation
33 Zhongshan Dong Yi Road, P.O. Box 253, Shanghai
Telephone: 232200
Telex: 33031 SITCO CN
Cable: INVESTCO SHANGHAI

US-China Business Council
1818 N. Street, NW, Suite 500
Washington, DC 20036
Telephone: 202 429-0340.
Fax: 202 775-2476

4

◆

The Work Setting

The Chinese Work Force

Modern China's labor force is primarily permanent and government-directed. The government dictates where a person will work upon graduation from school. Pay, hours worked, reasons for dismissal, and working conditions are also determined by governmental agencies. Hiring is done through a municipal agency that allots new workers according to need and national policy. However, all school graduates needing work are given positions irrespective of demand, and most collective work units (*danweis*) have at least a 20 percent redundancy in their labor forces.

Hiring and Firing Practices

The Contract System regulation, which allows foreign ventures to hire and fire their workers, was passed in 1986. Under the 1986 law, workers theoretically are expected to sign individual work contracts with their employers, though actual practices seldom meet this standard. These contracts vary in length from three to five or more years. There nevertheless remains great reluctance on the part of work units, labor unions, and the Communist Party to accept the practice of individual contracts, even though these contracts are usually negotiated by labor officials, who remain mediators and shadow employers with indirect but significant influence.

The most common hiring practice is to offer foreigners a collective labor contract for a group of workers. The contract defines the employment terms, wages, social security and other benefits, working hours, and so forth. Usually, the foreign employer has limited power in hiring and firing procedures, and these must be negotiated very carefully. At times, even the number of workers in a proposed package is determined by labor officials rather than by the prospective foreign employer.

It is possible for a foreign partner to give the Chinese partner all responsibility for recruiting, training, and supervising all workers and managers. Most foreign partners, however, prefer to maintain some control over selection and dismissals, though control will always be limited. In such cases, some Western compensation and work rules policies can be instituted, and these are negotiated when the labor package is considered.

Foreigners who are able to control to some degree the work rules, performance criteria, dismissals, and bonuses of their local workers are more likely to gain their loyalty. Individual workers are motivated to be more productive when they realize that their actions will determine the amount of their pay. However, no foreign employer in China will have the relative freedom enjoyed in the capitalist West. Individual reward systems remain Western practices not always condoned by the Chinese. Few Chinese managers want to award bonuses to individuals on the basis of merit or productivity. The practice of equal rewards to all members of a work team remains a central tenet of Chinese managers.

The procedures for recruiting and dismissal illustrate the limitations placed on foreign joint-venture partners. For example, Chinese universities do not allow foreigners to recruit graduates directly. Instead, recruiters submit a list of their labor needs to the local employment department. Only then will a match be attempted to meet the needs of recruiter and applicant. The foreigner is not allowed to freely interview any prospective graduate on the campus. The most common procedure is for the labor department to send qualified applicants for interviews.

Joint-venture partners, and foreigners in general, cannot dismiss workers at will. Workers can usually (though not always) be dismissed as a result of technological changes that make them superfluous, and new workers who cannot learn proper procedures after joining a training program sometimes can be dismissed. Workers also can be dismissed when they violate work or safety rules causing "bad consequences." Generally, however, redundant workers cannot be dismissed.

The conditions for dismissals are vaguely defined. They must be clearly stated in the contracts and should be carefully negotiated. Regardless of the reasons for dismissal, such workers must be compensated, based on length of employment. All dismissals must be accepted by the local labor union. Most discharges are resolved through mediation and extensive negotiation.

Power Structures in Chinese Organizations

Before the reforms of the early 1980s, foreign businesspersons dealt only with Chinese state officials. These officials acted as intermediaries between buyers and sellers. Foreigners seldom met their Chinese suppliers or buyers face-to-face. There is still some attempt to "protect" Chinese entrepreneurs from direct interaction with foreigners, but this practice is no longer mandatory.

Export-import decision making has now been decentralized. Foreign negotiators can almost always deal directly with their Chinese counterparts. Although state officials are still involved in business dealings with foreigners, they generally do so indirectly, and they always are shadow partners in joint ventures. It is therefore necessary that foreigners understand Chinese organizational structures. Organizations in China—whether industrial or not—have both Asian and socialistic characteristics. These features make Chinese organizations unique in many respects.

General Managers and Cadres

The highest rank in a Chinese manufacturing organization is the general manager (*chang-zhang*). Before 1983, the local secretary of the Communist Party (*danwei shuji*) held veto power on all decisions. In theory, the general manager now has the most authority. Whether this is actually so varies from organization to organization and according to changing government policy and varying political situations. In recent years, the party secretary has gained in influence in relation to the general manager.

In principle, the general manager is elected by the Workers' Representative Congress. In fact, the general manager has almost complete control in the selection of the managerial candidate and is generally self-selected. The general manager appoints all other senior-level managers. These persons—called *cadres*—can control any other election of senior and mid-level managers, especially those supported by local party representatives.

In some factories, the general manager may dominate the party secretary because of the manager's dominant personality or personal connections with high-level officials or party members. The party secretary nevertheless has great potential power and retains a high degree of informal authority. The party also continues to control a number of policies that affect workers and managers, such as how much time workers should spend studying Communist ideology during workdays.

For example, the American managers in charge of the AMC-Beijing Automotive Works joint venture decided to ignore the local party secretary and his associates. However, every shop and department had party members—roughly three hundred out of four thousand workers—and the party secretary and his assistants were serving as a "shadow" organization within the more formal structure of the company. Consequently, each major decision made in the joint venture was scrutinized by party officials. After recognizing this situation, AMC (now Chrysler) officials opened channels of communication for consultation with the party secretary and other party representatives.

Party Power and Influence

Local Communist officials also oversee the administrative policies of the party. At the AMC-Beijing plant, Jim Mann recounts that party officials enforced the "one-child" policy. They demanded that workers or their wives who gave birth to a second child have their wages reduced 40 percent. There was also the hidden (from the Americans) policy of awarding a bonus of two-months' wages to women workers with one child who aborted their second pregnancies.[1] The party's influence remains pervasive. These labor costs and policies were outside the control of the American partners.

The party still maintains partial control over wages. Foreign managers normally use bonuses to increase productivity by rewarding more productive workers. Individual reward systems, however, are not always condoned by the Chinese, who consider them individualistic Western practices not in accord with socialist principles. Bonuses, which in China can amount to a pay increase of 50 percent or more, create inequalities between the harder working employees and others. In China, bonuses have traditionally been awarded to all workers, regardless of behavior or productivity.

Consequently, the party secretary can ask a rewarded worker to "volunteer" to donate some or most of a bonus to the labor union's welfare fund. This practice is common when Chinese managers earn pay or receive individual performance-based bonuses that are much higher than average. Although this practice may ensure equality, it also destroys individual initiative and productivity.

General Manager Responsibility System

Theoretically, most Chinese enterprises now follow a *general manager responsibility system* in which upper-level executives and managers are expected to manage their firms in a profitable manner. The system was established to encourage managers to use their initiative to gain profits from their organizations. The profits are then distributed to the workers according to rank. This arrangement is increasingly found in joint ventures with foreigners. The real authority of the general manager varies extensively, however.

In the past, no organization in China was expected to earn a "profit" in the Western economic sense. The responsibility of managers was to produce whatever the current national five-year plan demanded, regardless of cost and usually of quality. All year-end profits were given to the state. The concept of "profit" is still poorly understood and has little emphasis in most state-owned enterprises, which include nearly all firms in China, especially the large-scale manufacturing and urban factories. At present, most state-owned factories and enterprises operate at a loss.

Workers have little official authority in Chinese firms, and they are allowed little decision-making power. However, their greatest input is in the selection of their immediate superiors—the foremen— since supervisors in Chinese factories are elected by the workers. The workers' wishes, however, are not absolute, and workers' power to determine supervisors has decreased in recent years.

The significance for foreigners is that they must deal with a large number of managers before anyone will commit to a course of action. The situation becomes a little simpler when a person is able to hold more than one post. General managers who are also first or second secretaries of the local Communist Party committee are those with the greatest influence.

Other powerful cadres (leaders) are those known to have close connections with powerful government officials or other managers. These persons are able to use their personal connections to encourage the relevant bureaucracies to make decisions, obtain scarce supplies, and so forth.

The general manager appoints all of the cadres, and the party secretary controls appointments to the higher ranks in the party, Youth League, and Labor Union. Members of these groups are loyal to their superiors. Work organizations can be defined as groups of persons in which each position-holder is personally dependent on the superior at the next organizational level.

The general manager is aided by vice general managers who are responsible for various specialized areas: production, finance (accounts), sales, and so forth. Each vice general manager is responsible for one or more workshops or divisions, each in turn led by directors. The general manager may have one or more assistants.

The general manager, vice general managers, and assistants are essentially the cadres or decision makers in Chinese organizations. Their influence, however, is more comprehensive than that of their Western counterparts from the viewpoint of the workers. Chinese cadres are responsible for the living standard of the workers as well as for their work-related behavior. While few managers have absolute power in terms of the work behavior, they nevertheless have almost total influence on the daily, nonwork aspects of the workers' lives.

Party Secretaries and Their Power

The functions of the party secretary have been discussed. However, foreigners need to be acutely aware of the secretary's powers. Party secretaries were stripped of their administrative powers in 1988 in order to give general managers, who are appointed to their positions because of their work-related talents and experience, more freedom to conduct their businesses without political interference.

However, the degree of independence general managers enjoy varies with prevailing political policies. China's leaders remain skeptical of capitalism and the possible benefits of a market-driven economy. A recent article reported that the party secretary of a factory with 35,000 workers had been reinstalled along with 340 party members in order to increase the political activities of workers.[2] Once again, all managerial decisions were to be made jointly with party officials. The latter, of course, hold their positions because of their political orthodoxy rather than for their work-related skills.

In this instance, politics has reemerged as the dominant element. As the party secretary noted, "From now on, the factory director won't be the only one who calls the shots. It's necessary for factory managers to share power with the party to make sure that the factory won't veer off the socialist track and become capitalist."[3]

At a minimum, the reestablishment of the Communist Party in businesses means that workers are expected to join study groups during working hours to discuss the decline of world capitalism, the central importance of China's Communist Party, and the correct ideological position.

Such changes in policy—asserting politics over business—result in decreased productivity. But the practices are mandatory regardless of contractual conditions. All managers (cadres) as well as line workers are expected to study political texts and join discussion groups. Managers may take time off from work themselves to study for a series of examinations on political topics and ideology.

Line workers in many factories, often indicate their political enthusiasm by taking part in revolutionary song contests.[4] These sessions take place during the workday, further decreasing productivity. When called upon, these singing workers take time off to compete in song contests against other factory choirs and to show their talents in various demonstrations. The manufacturing organization is expected to meet the costs of these events. Not doing so indicates the cadres are counterrevolutionary and disloyal.

Bureaucratic Communication

Chinese bureaucracies are organized as hierarchies. The leadership structure is top-to-bottom, and subordinates are rarely given any autonomy. Leadership is generally authoritarian, and subordinates are not expected to use their initiative.

To get things done in China, it is necessary to adopt a top-level strategy: deal with as many high-level managers and officials as possible. This means establishing relationships with general managers rather than with their subordinates.

Little lateral communication exists in Chinese bureaucracies and divisions. Communication channels primarily facilitate vertical (top-to-bottom) exchanges with relatively little communication or coordination across divisions. Visualize, if you will, the typical Chinese organization as a series of pyramids, with little communication from one pyramid to another. Thus, each department becomes an isolated mini-empire.

Bureaucratic divisions are also very secretive. Knowledge is a source of power and prestige, and officials do not give out information easily. Foreigners obtain most information through personal contacts (*guanxi*). A high-ranking foreigner may have easier access to the leaders of many divisions or "pyramids." If the venture has high priority, various leaders will be willing to help the foreigner. In such situations, foreigners may receive aid and communication from a number of sources and, therefore, will be better informed than are their Chinese counterparts and co-managers. Foreigners also have access to information from their embassies, which often develop excellent networks of information and resources.

Attitudes Toward Managers

Socialist and traditional values in China hold that managers do not create wealth; only workers create wealth or add anything valuable to society by their labor. Since wealth is created only by workers, in an ideal work setting, managers would not accept any rewards for their work. That is, managerial salaries by definition belong to the workers, and such incomes are exploitative. In addition, workers owe little in exchange for their salaries and other benefits. In a socialist factory, workers are owed living wages because they are members of the society, not because they are productive. Foreign managers cannot assume that simply because they are managers they can demand higher productivity and quality work from their workers

Managers, especially foreign managers and executives, are held in low esteem in China. Their function is not to work for private gain but to serve the workers and China as a nation. Managers, therefore, should be more concerned for the workers' welfare than for their own or for that of the firm—the workers' needs come first. In China, the ideal manager is paternalistic rather than efficient or productive.

To be effective, foreign managers should learn to couch their demands in group terms: a plan will help the workers rather than the firm. Another strategy is to suggest that increased efficiency will result in the firm's ability to provide better housing, or whatever else is needed, for the workers. Foreign managers also need to learn how to balance the workers' needs with the needs of the firm. The ideal manager, from a Chinese point of view, is one who offers special benefits in addition to basic wages and bonuses. It is customary for Chinese managers and workers to exchange favors. On the manager's side, workers are allowed to sleep on the job, read newspapers, or leave work to shop. In exchange, workers are expected—

for a while—to work hard to meet a specific deadline or to be concerned about quality output.

Foreign managers must develop good personal relationships with Chinese colleagues and subordinates. They cannot assume that rank and position automatically give them the authority to give orders that will be obeyed. Good managers in China build up personal credits with workers by granting favors. The workers then become personally loyal to a manager and repay the favors with greater efforts— by becoming more productive, more careful with their tools and machines, and so forth.

Chinese managers, on the other hand, often assume that *all* managerial behavior is paternalistic, inefficient, and emphasizes personal relationships over the company's interests. They extrapolate from their own experiences and assume that foreign managers also will not become upset by delays, personal favoritism, and worker inefficiency.

While foreign managers must work within the Chinese cultural context, they also have the opportunity to educate Chinese managers and colleagues by showing them how foreign work patterns are different from those common in China. Foreigners must become teachers and should be patient with Chinese ways of managing and working.

The *Danwei* Work Unit

The central social unit in today's Chinese society, apart from the family, is the *danwei* work unit. *Danweis* are found primarily in the urban areas. All work organizations, such as factory complexes, department stores, hospitals, or schools, are organized as *danweis*.

Danweis are urban communes. They form what sociologists call "total institutions" that provide total support for their members. The *danwei* influences all aspects of an individual's life. Foreigners cannot understand modern China without a clear understanding of the nature of the *danwei* and its importance in the lives of modern-day Chinese.

The all-pervasive significance of a person's *danwei* is indicated by the fact that some members submerge their identities into their *danweis*. When meeting new persons, the Chinese may first ask strangers what their *danwei* is and then will ask a person's name. Workers also may call themselves by their *danwei's* name ("I am *danwei* Beijing Electric Works"). The *danwei* is first of all a work unit that varies in size. A large steel-producing complex, for example, may have ten thousand or more members. Most *danweis* are much smaller.

Young adults are assigned to a *danwei* after completing their education. The individual usually has little choice in employers. A local municipal agency has the responsibility to match employment needs according to national goals and individual talents. Most assignments are not overly concerned with an individual's preferences. Under Communist ideology, a person works for the good of China, for Communism, or for the people. Working only with one's interests in mind is seen as selfish. It is a person's duty to willingly go to a *danwei* selected by others. One of the demands of the 1989 demonstrators at Tiananmen Square was to end involuntary *danwei* assignments after graduation.

Once assigned to a *danwei*, the individual must remain a member until retirement. A worker may resign a position to work in the free market but by doing so will lose all privileges such as medical insurance and retirement benefits. A worker who wants to change employers must be formally released by the current *danwei* and formally accepted by the *new* unit. The current *danwei* need not give permission for a transfer. Permission will not be given if the individual has valuable skills useful to the *danwei*. Sometimes a transferee pays the *danwei* a lump sum, as repayment for educational and other costs, in order to receive the *danwei's* permission to change membership.

Having become a member of a *danwei*, the individual is given a job. He or she is also given housing, free or subsidized meals, hospitalization, food products at a discount, and so forth. Some of the larger *danweis* operate small stores, barber shops, schools for the members' children, and other services. These services are so comprehensive that relatively few exist outside the *danwei* system. As a result, foreigners living in China are cut off from most of these amenities.

The most important services *danweis* offer are housing and scarce commodities such as meat, salt, cotton cloth, bicycles, or television sets. A good *danwei* manager obtains goods that are not found in state-run stores and markets. The University of Beijing *danwei*, for example, publishes textbooks, provides inexpensive food for students and faculty, a bicycle repair shop, a movie theater, two hospitals, schools for the children of staff and faculty, a tailor, and other amenities.

Larger *danweis* have their own food departments, their own hospitals, and even colleges for the workers' children. Workers who need funds can receive loans or grants from the *danwei's* bank. The *danwei* will pay for the special educational needs of the members' children.

Larger *danweis* support extensive medical facilities. *Danweis* that do not have adequate facilities send members to hospital *danweis* and pay most of the cost. Members also receive subsidized housing. When funds and materials are available, *danweis* subsidize workers who wish to renovate their homes or buy new housing away from the *danwei.*

During holiday seasons, *danweis* purchase or produce holiday foods for sale or assignment to families. Some *danweis* have purchased housing at vacation spots for their members. Members traveling during holidays or visiting family members are usually subsidized by their *danweis.*

Danweis also support their members after retirement. Essentially, *danweis* are concerned with every detail of members' lives, from cradle to grave, in a combination of a traditional Chinese extended family and the ideals of socialism.

The *danwei's* significance is amply illustrated by the Panzhihua Iron & Steel Co. *danwei*, a work unit of 55,000 workers and families. The *danwei* supports a 500-bed hospital and eight clinics. Those needing additional medical care are sent to more specialized facilities at no personal cost. The *danwei* also operates a television station and publishes its own newspaper, in part because the factory is located in an isolated area with no nearby cities.[5]

There is a *danwei*-supported bus system, plus 59 cafeterias where the cost of food is subsidized. Those wishing to eat at home can purchase some of the 80 million tons of produce made available each year at cost, or about half the cost charged in the open markets. For holidays, the *danwei* offers special foods, including fresh crabs gathered over a thousand miles away.

The *danwei's* Youth Organization organizes dances and supports a dance band. Party representatives offer lectures on family planning and birth control. Most of the workers' furniture is made by *danwei* carpenters, as is all the housing. The cultural center has a swimming pool, coffee shops, and rooms for social and political activities, including a library. There are *danwei*-supported schools from kindergarten through high school.

The members' ten thousand children are guaranteed employment at the steel works when they enter the labor force, even if there is no demand for their labor. All workers maintain most benefits and housing after retirement, and they are cremated by the company after death.

The *danwei* is led by the general manager, with the assistance of the local secretaries of the Communist Party, Youth League, and labor union. The responsibilities of the Youth League include cultural and athletic activities, assigning movie tickets, and political education. The labor union leaders are responsible for the general welfare of the workers, including the distribution of bonuses, promotions, retirement benefits, and safety and work procedures. Representatives of these organizations visit the sick, mediate disputes, and support morale. A wife who feels she is being mistreated by her husband will complain to a local committee or its representatives, since *danwei* administrators are responsible for members' behavior.

Because society at large defines a person in terms of *danwei* membership, those who do not belong to *danweis* are isolated and helpless before China's numerous bureaucracies. When the police arrest someone, they will call the person's *danwei* first and often will deal with the *danwei* administrators rather than with the accused. A *danwei* with influence can help a member avoid a trial and almost certain imprisonment.

The significance of *danwei* membership is often ignored by foreigners. Chinese workers, employed by a foreign company as part of a joint venture or because they have been "loaned" to a foreign firm, maintain their major loyalty to their *danweis*. Motivating Chinese workers lies with the *danweis*, not with their foreign employers. *Danwei* officials determine wages, bonuses, working conditions, and other facets of employment. In fact, the wages paid by foreign employers are turned over to a state agency, which in turn allocates a certain amount to the workers' *danweis*. The *danwei* then gives each worker a basic allowance and retains the rest. Since foreign employers may pay three to ten times the average rate for workers, this provides a substantial profit for the *danweis*.

This arrangement makes the employer-employee relationship different in China than it is in the West. Foreigners deal with *danweis* rather than with individuals. No venture in China will be successful unless the foreigner works with the *danwei* structures.

In many ways, *danweis* are government-directed agencies. *Danwei* administrators must follow state directives, even if the local *danweis* must pay the cost. One observer reports that the AMC-Beijing automotive works *danwei* gave workers time off when party officials demanded increased study sessions on socialist theory.[6]

This *danwei* (and all others) was expected to give bonuses to women workers who had undergone sterilizations after having one child or who promised not to have more than one child. Workers also must be given bonuses and travel expenses when they attend functions such as government-sponsored demonstrations, parades, or Communist Party regional meetings.

Difficult **Danwei** *Policies*

From a foreign employer's perspective, the most damaging policies of the *danweis* are (1) "latent unemployment" and (2) the "iron rice bowl." The term *latent unemployment* refers to the large number of workers in various work units who are not needed. Estimates are that at least one-half of China's urban workers are excess labor and not needed in the positions they hold. This is the result of the full employment policy of the government that *danweis* are expected carry out regardless of the inefficiencies this policy entails. *Danweis* are allocated members to ensure full employment even when additional workers are not requested or needed. These form the surplus labor of the *danwei*. Foreigners have to expect at least a 20 percent redundancy in their Chinese labor force, and the figure is usually higher.

Only very few ventures are given complete independence to hire exactly the types and numbers of workers needed. *Danweis* may overcharge for their workers who are sent to a foreign venture. The surcharges then support the excess workers in the *danwei* unit. Foreigners as a result pay for excess labor directly or indirectly.

The *iron rice bowl* concept refers to the complete job security offered by the *danweis*. An iron rice bowl cannot be broken and ensures a constant food supply. *Danweis* cannot dismiss excess or inadequate workers. Those dismissed would have no housing, no income, and no other benefits. The government cannot take care of these isolated individuals because Chinese socialism operates primarily through the *danwei* network.

Housing Scarcity

A very scarce commodity in China is housing. Exhibit 4-1 contrasts the size of housing in China and selected provinces to that in other countries. The standard for housing space in China is 4 square meters per person, small by any standards. Yet roughly 15 percent of the people in China's cities live in housing with an average space of less than 4 square meters per person.

It is now illegal to move to China's urban areas unless a person has both a job and housing. Those without jobs usually move in with already-crowded relatives or friends, which is illegal. At present, 80 percent of all new housing is bought or financed by *danweis*. Persons who are not part of a *danwei* find that housing is either unavailable or too expensive. The only available housing for non-*danwei* adults is to live with family members; thus, family connections are important sources of support.

One hindrance to job mobility is that persons who change *danweis* must also change housing, since almost all urban housing in China belongs either to the government or to *danweis*. A *danwei* could not attract new workers unless it could offer housing. One major barrier to marriage among young adults is the lack of housing. Many couples delay marriage until their *danweis* can offer them their own apartments.

Excess Workers

A few years ago, factory *danweis* were allowed to "encourage" part of their membership to leave and seek employment in other *danweis* or in the free market. Some members were encouraged to stay home rather than work. However, these members were paid 70 percent of their work wages. Some could also keep their housing and other benefits.

The rationale for this plan was that at least a factory would not have idle workers at the plant reading newspapers, standing idle, or taking naps. Chinese factories have more workers than machines, so there are always too many workers for the work available. Excess workers often disappear for several hours to shop, visit friends, or stand in line at markets to obtain scarce commodities. The push to allow workers to seek employment outside their *danweis* was devel-

---

Exhibit 4-1. International Comparisons of Urban Housing
(Square meters per person)

	Meters	Year		Meters	Year
West Germany	25	(1978)	Beijing	5.7	(1983)
France	13	(1976)	Zhejiang	5.6	(1983)
United States	18	(1976)	Hunan	5.4	(1983)
Japan	13	(1978)	Yunan	5.3	(1983)
Singapore	15	(1980)	Liaoning	3.0	(1983)

oped in the hope of reducing the numbers of idle factory workers. This plan has not yet been particularly successful.

The issue of excess workers continues to be a problem. Since full employment is a central policy of China's government, few foreigners are able to streamline their work force and reduce labor costs to a minimum.

A worker who is in demand by foreigners because of language or occupational skills may not be released unconditionally by the worker's *danwei*. Instead, the person will be "on loan" for a period of time. However, the *danwei* can recall loaned workers pretty much at will. The foreign employer usually has little choice in the matter.

In fact, the search for a stable, well-trained Chinese labor force demands that the foreign employer develop the resources of a *danwei*. Such a decision, however, demands a large investment at the start of the venture and a long-term commitment to stay in China.

Labor Costs

We have already discussed the fact that labor costs are dependent on many factors outside a foreigner's control. However, a number of general principles guide labor cost projections to some extent. A major goal of China's leaders is to raise wages and the standard of living while maintaining as much equality as possible.

A major tenet of Chinese Communism is wealth equality. Any policy that undermines this principle meets resistance. Bonuses, for example, are awarded on a group level, often according to rank. Offering bonuses to individuals as a reward for individual productivity is considered non-Communist.

This principle of wealth equality causes a number of problems for foreign employers. One author notes that foreign managers stationed in China receive at least $50,000 annually plus special bonuses.[7] This amount, however, is roughly one hundred times the pay of managers in Chinese enterprises. Thus paying Chinese managers at the same rate as foreign managers creates unacceptable inequalities among the Chinese.

Most joint ventures pay their Chinese managers the standard wage plus a personal bonus. Increasing pay levels to international levels would be prohibitive for most Western companies and would also eliminate much of their reason to be in China. A partial solution is to offer a Chinese worker the standard pay plus at least 20 percent.

This avoids having a group of workers in foreign-owned enterprises earning much higher pay than those working in Chinese national firms. To obtain an added source of income, various governmental agencies tax excess pay extremely heavily. A general manager working for a foreign joint venture generally is asked to forfeit 25 percent or more of excess pay to support unspecified welfare costs.

Pay Structure

Industrial workers are usually paid according to an 8-grade pay system, but the pay differences from one pay level to another are relatively slight. Pay is heavily influenced by seniority and age.

The pay for grade 8 workers is three times that of grade 1 (entry level) workers. Only about 2 percent of industrial workers achieve grade 8. All workers, however, receive more or less the same benefits, which are more important than their actual wages. Even a factory general manager lives in a two- or three-room apartment, the same as other workers. Other benefits, such as medical services, are distributed on a fairly equal basis.

Exhibit 4-2 lists the pay structures in three industries in China during 1984. The 1986 average monthly income of an industrial worker was US$121.[8] As Exhibit 4-2 indicates, monthly salaries, excluding bonuses, are fairly evenly distributed across ranks. The higher rankings receive higher bonuses, but the differences are not great, since bonuses seldom account for more than 25 percent of base salary.

Exhibit 4-2. Average Pay by Rank and Industry
(In Yuan per Month)

| | Industry | | |
Rank	Steel	Glass	Textile
Corporate Manager	150-290	150-160	100
General Manager	100-150	80-90	100
Workshop Manager	100	70	60-70
Group Leader	100	60	50-60
Factory Worker	65	50	55

Source: Adapted from Oiva Laaksonen, *Management in China During and After Mao in Enterprises, Government, and Party* (Berlin and New York: Walter de Gruyter, 1988), 259.

Corporate managers in the steel industry receive a base pay that is no more than five times the wage of line workers. This range is extreme when compared to those in other industries, where pay differentials are much lower.

Nonindustrial urban workers, such as professionals, government officials, or engineers, form about half of the urban labor force. They are subject to other pay scales. Government administrators have a 26-grade scale, with the highest grade receiving fifteen times that of the lowest level. This range is larger than those of other pay scales. Higher government officials also receive much better fringe benefits, such as special stores and subsidized vacations.

The average monthly labor costs during the late 1980s for Chinese who worked for foreigners was about $95.50.[9] The worker actually received $45.00 in take-home pay. The rest consisted of various taxes, welfare contributions, medical, housing, and retirement payments.

However, the actual charges to foreign employers are always higher than the estimated labor costs, which are higher than for Chinese enterprises. A 1986 Chinese law specifies that foreign-invested enterprises must pay wages not lower than 120 percent of the "average wage," which is in turn loosely defined and must be negotiated. In 1986, foreigners paid an average of $1,220 per month for each local worker, a charge of roughly 1,200 percent over local wage levels. This "service fee," as it is often called, is negotiable but foreigners always pay a premium for hiring Chinese labor.[10]

Additional labor costs are generally minor. Depending on local conditions, workers receive a number of small subsidies, including travel, rent, heating, sanitation, and sometimes food allowances. These subsidies generally add 15 percent to the worker's basic wage.

Foreign-owned enterprises also pay subsidies to the local government for services used by the workers. Subsidies may include food and fuel provided by municipal agencies and vary by location. The subsidies also vary if local officials believe they can enforce an arbitrary increase. The proper reaction is for the foreigner or the Chinese partner to complain and seek mediation.

Foreign-owned enterprises deposit at least 7.4 percent of the monthly wage bill to a medical care fund. Insurance and welfare taxes take another 20 percent. Some of these taxes are received by the workers in the form of subsidies for such items as haircuts, death benefits, or bonuses for family size restrictions.

Labor insurance and medical costs range up to 48 percent of base wages. There are also donations to welfare and bonus funds that are turned over to the local labor union. Sometimes bonuses are taxed by the local provincial and municipal governments.

Other taxes (donations) are based on current policy and location. The goal of foreigners is to negotiate as much autonomy as possible for all labor costs. Not paying careful attention to these financial details can make China's labor costs relatively expensive when compared to those in other Asian countries.

Foreigners, especially Americans, often tolerate payment abuses in order to stay in China.[11] This passiveness is not necessary. The Chinese are eager to gain all the foreign currency they can from foreigners, but they are also willing to negotiate. Careful preparation and knowledge of local conditions are necessary, however, or labor costs will increase drastically.

In recent years, the central government has regained some control of bonus payments made by foreign employers by taxing the bonuses. While the ability to give bonuses has been decentralized to give more authority to local and municipal bureaucracies, the issue is a major concern to China's Communist leaders. Their reaction is to discourage bonuses to individuals as much as possible or else to receive some financial gain from the practice.

Some central authorities have established taxes of 30 percent on bonuses that are in excess of four months of wage equivalent; 100 percent, in excess of five months; and 300 percent, in excess of six months. These are negotiable from location to location.[12]

As mentioned earlier, material rewards are more useful to individual workers than are cash bonuses. Allowing workers who surpass a certain quota to take an extra holiday is an alternative to cash bonuses. Managers can distribute theater tickets or food vouchers instead of cash. The company can also distribute scarce goods to the more productive workers, including television sets, bicycles, watches, or flashlights. Extra cloth to make clothes is always welcomed.

Doing business in China offers challenges and frustrations not found elsewhere. In a study of the sources of stress experienced by foreigners stationed in China, the Organization of Resources Counselors, Inc. concludes its report with the following:

[T]he position of the multinational with respect to Chinese human resources is almost tragi-comic. To exaggerate only slightly: you can't hire; you can't fire; you can't discipline; individual incentives are frowned upon;

retention of good workers is largely, if not completely, out of your hands; you may not even know who is working for you exactly or how much you are paying them because all the books are being kept in Chinese; your workers have the legal right to form a union whether you like it or not, and...the union is run by the party and the party boss happens to be your co-manager—or so you suspect. While these circumstances are certainly different, they are really not unmanageable. What is needed is a different set of skills and a lot of different knowledge.[13]

Trade Unions

Joint ventures are required to sign contracts with the trade union. Trade union officials are responsible for setting wage levels, defining working conditions, and so forth. They supervise the implementation of all labor conditions as set by national and local directives.

Local union officials have to be notified whenever a worker is to be disciplined or dismissed. They are also concerned with bonus distributions, leaves and absences, and similar work-related situations. Workers with complaints against their employers expect union officials to redress their grievances.

One hidden labor cost for larger enterprises is the legal requirement that companies release a specified number of workers for full-time union activities, depending on the size of the company's work force. Exhibit 4-3 lists the number of union officials on the union's steering committee that must be released from work.

After the 4,001 level is reached, an additional worker is released for every 2,000 employees. The employer also provides a meeting place and other facilities for the trade union at no cost. While union meetings are usually held after work hours, it is wise to allow some meetings during the workday. The number of meetings allowable is a matter for negotiation.

Exhibit 4-3. Workers Required for Union Activities

Number of Staff and Workers	Number Released for Full-Time Union Activities
200-500	1
501-1,000	2
1,001-1,500	3
1,501-2,500	4
2,501-4,000	5

Unions in China do not automatically adopt an adversarial role vis-à-vis management. They can be valuable mechanisms to settle disputes, distribute bonuses, arrange holiday events, organize sports and other leisure activities, and so forth. But trade unions are agencies of the central government, so they also oversee the government's regulations and protect its interests. Unions can also be effective in raising productivity. In fact, no policy aimed at retraining or upgrading skills or productivity will be successful unless supported by union officials. According to a report published by the Organization Resources Counselors, Inc., trade unions have generally been very cooperative with foreign venture partners.[14] Union officials usually maintain close contacts with party official and other cadres and are useful sources of influence.

Many unions exist primarily as social clubs, though they also help maintain safety and health regulations. Unions are highly involved, however, whenever workers are threatened with dismissals. A worker cannot be dismissed unless the local trade union approves, and most union officials hesitate to agree to the need for most dismissals. Such caution makes the process to dismiss a worker lengthy (often a year or more) unless the foreign partner has received broad powers of dismissal in the firm's contract. Even then, dismissals and demotions are very delicate issues, and managers cannot dismiss workers at will.

Time Schedules in the Work Setting

The official workweek is 48 hours. Usually, workers stop working on Saturday at noon, so the actual number of hours that workers are at their workplace is less than that. In addition, the Communist Party sponsors study groups on Saturday afternoons. These are mandatory and outside the control of a foreign employer's influence. Foreign managers are not allowed to attend such meetings, in order to keep meeting deliberations secret. During times of political tension, as from 1989 to 1991, workers were expected to stop work periodically to attend extra study sessions.

It is difficult to extend the workweek through overtime. Chinese workers do not enjoy working overtime. They may see the workday as long enough, and much of a worker's leisure time is spent shopping or dealing with government agencies. In a land with a large surplus population, overtime is seen as selfish and exploitative and as benefiting only a few. Workers are paid a government-mandated time-and-a-half. Overtime excess earnings are often taxed formally through taxation or informally through "voluntary" donations to the trade union's welfare fund.

Increased production is better-achieved through increased productivity. Manufacturers should be prepared for delays, since overtime can seldom be used to make up for missed deadlines caused by delays in supply deliveries, power shortages, or other unexpected events.

Sunday is the near-universal day off. In order to stagger industrial electric use, some factories operate on Sundays, however, and those who work then are given another designated holiday. Retail stores are open on Sundays, and the clerks' days off are staggered to maintain a constant labor force throughout the week.

In most cases, the workday begins at eight o'clock in the morning and ends at five o'clock in the afternoon, with a one-hour lunch break at noon. In some *danweis*, workers are allowed a half-hour lunch break so that they can leave earlier. Many, especially cadres, take additional time for a nap. There are two official fifteen-minute breaks at 10:00 a.m. and 4:00 p.m. each day. These are counted as part of the workload and are mandated by national policy.

Most *danwei* administrators are flexible about workers' actual working hours. It is usually possible to take extra time off to shop, accompany children to or from school, transport an item to the *danwei's* repair shop, or to conduct other personal business.

The Nap Syndrome

Apart from China's bureaucratic red tape, overemployment, and inefficient (or absent) workers, foreigners find the Chinese practice of taking noon naps a most irritating practice. Most administrators and many workers take short naps after lunch. Napping (*xiu-xi*) is a very traditional custom and an important occupational perk denoting prestige and rank. The Chinese national constitution guarantees a midday work rest, which includes the right to a nap. Employees often eat lunch early so they can enjoy a longer nap.

To set aside enough time for both lunch and nap, most offices close around 11:00 a.m. and reopen at 2:00 p.m. or so. Longer naps (up to three hours) are taken in the summer and shorter naps (one hour or so), during the winter. Administrative offices include beds or sofas for napping as standard equipment. The custom is so ingrained as a part of the workday that it is hard to completely end the practice. It is also an integral part of medical mythology: it is believed that those who cannot nap lose their energy to work in the late afternoon and that they are sick more often.

The Chinese explain that naps replenish one's energies for the afternoon's work. Napping is also seen as a health measure during the summer months. The temperatures in most of China's regions are high during the summer, and air conditioning is nearly nonexistent. Taking a nap during the hottest part of the day is defined as a health measure as well as a comfort. In some areas, air conditioners, as well as all electricity, are shut off to save energy or to provide more electricity to the factory floor. Workers are either sent home during this period or take naps until the blackouts are over.

The custom of taking naps is discouraged in many factories. Nor is it a worker's absolute right in some of China's cities and free economic zones. Some factory workers are giving up napping in exchange for a shorter workday. But in a country with excess labor, the practice of taking naps will disappear slowly, if at all.

Leaves From Work

Chinese workers are allowed a number of absences from work. One such absence is the *working leave,* which is an official absence taken for a specific, nonleisure purpose. Working leaves reflect the complete way of life in a *danwei* context. Working leaves may include going to a work-related or political exhibition in which members of a work team go as a group. Often, factory workers are taken off the job to take part in political demonstrations or to line the streets to welcome foreign dignitaries.

Other kinds of responsibilities also call for work leaves. Chinese hospitals and medical staffs expect most of the nonmedical care needed by patients to be met by the patients' families or by *danwei* members. These persons fix or serve meals, keep patients company, and care for them in general. Relatives or volunteers always are given paid working leaves to care for those hospitalized.

The second type of approved absence is *sick leave.* Those who become ill continue to receive all or most of their wages, except bonuses, while those in private, profit-oriented companies may lose their performance bonuses, which account for 50 to 70 percent of income. In state-owned enterprises, bonuses form only a small part of a worker's wages.

Those on sick leave for more than a year receive 70 percent of their base salary. Most patients must pay a small portion of their medical costs, so the long-term illness of a member can have grave consequences for a family's financial condition. The long-term ill, nevertheless, remain *danwei* members and receive various amounts of aid.

The third type of absence is *personal leave,* devoted to private matters. Personal leaves entail a reduction of pay and a forfeit of bonuses. Leaves that last less than four days usually do not involve any loss of pay. Personal leaves may include time for attending a wedding or funeral in a distant location or for a honeymoon.

Personal leaves also include vacations that last more than the officially-designated time. Vacations were first allowed during the early 1980s and were offered to workers with at least ten years seniority. Vacations are more common now and last from 10 to 20 days, according to seniority and rank.

Vacations are usually taken during the summer. Wealthier *danweis* sponsor trips to tourist attractions or subsidize tours, which are becoming very popular. Some *danweis* own hotels at the seashore for their members' use. Extra space is rented out to other *danweis.*

Holidays

A number of annual holidays, in addition to Sundays, result in a decrease in hours worked. The most important holiday is Spring Day or the *Chinese New Year,* which takes place in January or February, depending on the Chinese lunar calendar. The legal length of this holiday is four days, though actual celebrations begin at least two weeks before the official start. The work pace begins to slow as office parties and holiday preparations begin.

Business associates exchange gifts before the opening of the holiday, and most entertain each other at banquets and smaller parties. During the holiday itself, friends and colleagues visit each other's homes to eat and drink. Superiors and their subordinates often exchange visits at this time. These visits, conducted during the workday, necessarily slow work progress.

Many persons also take part in office parties and outings before and after Spring Day. Work teams may attend the theater or a movie together. Others take early leave to travel to other areas to visit relatives.

In addition to the Chinese New Years Day, other national holidays include May Day and National Day (October 1). These major holidays generally last two days, though productivity decreases for a longer time. There are other minor holidays that may or may not be observed.

Guanxi **Relationships**

The key to successful business dealings in China is *guanxi*. The term is defined as the special relationship between two persons. *Guanxi* can be translated as friendship with overtones of unlimited exchanges of favors. A *guanxi* relationship is between individuals, rather than between groups, and is a commitment to help the other person in practical matters. As a result, *guanxi* is established slowly and carefully over time as the partners exchange small gifts and learn to trust each other. Gradually, two persons begin to exchange more and greater favors.

All resources in China, except people, are limited. Scarce goods are exchanged through *guanxi* relationships. Foreigners who do not establish *guanxi* relationships will be unable to cut red tape or obtain goods outside official channels. These relationships must be continuously maintained. When they are not, a businessperson will find that Chinese officials are no longer willing to take a personal interest in proposed or ongoing projects.

A foreign businessperson in Beijing may need to fly to Shanghai the next day but may be told that all flights are booked. Yet, the person knows that tickets are almost always set aside for important officials. The foreigner then asks a Chinese friend whether tickets could be procured. That afternoon, the friend visits a cousin who works at CAAC, the organization that oversees domestic flights. The cousin agrees to set aside two tickets on a flight for the next day. The cousin will ask for a *guanxi* favor in the future. The friend then reports to the foreigner. Later, the friend will expect a favor in return. Someone who does not reciprocate loses face and is defined as selfish and undependable.

While *guanxi* relationships may involve feelings of friendship, such sentiments are not necessary. *Guanxi* is utilitarian rather than emotional. The necessary emotion in a *guanxi* relationship is trust that each partner will reciprocate for favors given earlier.

Guanxi relationships are also personal in that the relationships link individuals. Two persons involved in a *guanxi* relationship may exchange favors at work or in a personal context, or both. Much official business is conducted for personal—*guanxi*—reasons. A Canadian might help a Chinese friend get a son into a Canadian university by becoming the son's sponsor. The Chinese parent reciprocates by making certain that the Canadian friend receives an import license overnight rather than through the usual two-month process.

In this case, a personal favor was exchanged for a business favor.

In one actual case, a crate of valuable equipment was stored outdoors in the port area of Quanzhou, and no official wanted to take the responsibility for releasing the shipment. The importer managed to have a friend take the release forms to five separate offices to be stamped, and a month (or more) of paperwork was completed in one afternoon. The friend, of course, had *guanxi* relationships with the port officials.

Guanxi connections are especially helpful when hiring. Most Chinese managers do not know how to write reliable reference letters, since mid-career job mobility is a recent phenomenon in China. It is also difficult for a Chinese to criticize another person in an official document. While those hiring should resist employing *guanxi* hires who are relatives and close friends of the referring party, *guanxi* sources of recommendation can be valuable when few information sources for potential job applicants are available. The hirer must be clear that unacceptable hirees will be dismissed irrespective of their *guanxi* connections.[15]

Guanxi exchanges tend to favor the weaker member. If *guanxi* is established between two persons of unequal rank, the one who has more prestige or influence is responsible for giving more than he or she receives. According to Chinese Confucian moral standards, the stronger always helps the weaker. The weaker partner may ask for special favors but cannot repay them. In turn, the weaker partner does the best possible with the resources available. By the same token, a person who does more to help the weak gains face. The wealthy have the obligation to be magnanimous.

A consequence of this aspect of *guanxi* is that claims of inadequacy and inferiority should be taken with suspicion. People who acknowledge their own inferiority are suggesting that the superior party should make certain concessions. Offering effusive praise is one way to establish another person's relative superiority so that a favor can be expected.

In negotiating with the Chinese, Westerners find that they are expected to concede certain points because they come from a wealthier country. The Chinese assume that representatives of wealthy nations want to show their superiority by giving the poorer Chinese some advantages. Otherwise, the foreigners have rejected their *guanxi* responsibilities and thereby lose face.

The correct strategy when faced with such demands is for the foreigners to also plead poverty—to claim that the company is poor and that it is the Chinese who should be magnanimous. If this claim is not made, the Chinese negotiators may state that the foreigners are being arrogant and are insulting the People's Republic of China.

A practical consequence of *guanxi* is that personal loyalties are more important than organizational affiliations, bureaucratic procedures, or legal standards. A person's official rank or organizational position may not be indicative of power. A person of low rank may in fact be very influential because of *guanxi* relationships with those in higher positions.

As we noted earlier, little job mobility exists in China. Promotions are generally from within organizations. In a 1985 survey, 81 of the managers in 900 enterprises had worked in the same factories for over 10 years. The average time Chinese managers spend in the same enterprise is 18 years.[16]

Such long tenure in the same organization gives a manager opportunity to develop extensive *guanxi* ties with a large number of persons, and, in fact, managers and employees develop very strong ties and loyalty to one another. Such personal loyalties, based on *guanxi*, may be stronger than loyalty to the organization or to bureaucratic rules. Foreigners wishing to deal with the Chinese must develop *guanxi* relations themselves or know persons who enjoy *guanxi* with those in central positions. The development of one's own *guanxi* is preferable. Representatives of foreign businesses must therefore expect to stay in China for a long time in order to develop *guanxi* and to find out who has *guanxi* that can help in business relations. The challenge is to discover these influential persons or their associates. Otherwise, chances of business success are low.

Guanxi is anti-bureaucratic and pro-individual. Official policies change, but such changes may be unimportant if one has adequate *guanxi*. Policy in China is nearly always administered in flexible and personal ways. *Guanxi* is therefore supremely important, and no one can live successfully in China for any length of time without getting involved in *guanxi* relationships. Very little activity goes on that does not go faster or easier with *guanxi*.

Guanxi is prevalent because China is a land of scarcity. While the average Chinese is well-fed and clothed and has housing, adequate medical attention, and welfare security, most other resources are strained, and there are few available luxuries. The result is that anything beyond basic necessities—in effect, most consumer goods—is obtained through *guanxi* networks. In business, this is called "going through the back door" (*zou-hou-men*).

Because *guanxi* is second nature to the Chinese, they automatically extend this view to foreigners and assume that businesses in foreign countries also operate better with *guanxi* help. Chinese also assume that most foreigners in China are powerful persons who can perform *guanxi* favors.

Agreeing to help a Chinese with a problem is understood as an implicit promise that you have the power to solve a problem. You can say you will send for the correct university application form for a friend's daughter, but the Chinese friend is likely to assume that you are also saying you have influence with the admissions office. Promises to do favors must be carefully explained so that the person does not lose face if the promises cannot be delivered.

Endnotes

1. Jim Mann, *Beijing Jeep: The Short, Unhappy Romance of American Business in China* (New York: Simon and Schuster, 1989).
2. Julia Leung, "Party Secretaries Emerge as Power Brokers," *Asian Wall Street Journal,* 1 January 1990,
3. Ibid.
4. Ibid.
5. Adi Ignatius, *Asian Wall Street Journal,* 3 October 1989, and *Wall Street Journal,* 17 October 1989.
6. Mann, *Beijing Jeep.*
7. Margaret M. Pearson, "The Erosion of Controls Over Foreign Capital in China, 1979-1988: Having Their Cake and Eating It Too?" *Modern China,* January 1991: 112-150.
8. Oiva Laaksonen, *Management in China During and After Mao in Enterprises, Government, and Party* (Berlin and New York: Walter de Gruyter, 1988).
9. Jamie P. Horsley, "The Chinese Workforce," *China Business Review* (May-June 1988): 50-55.
10. Ibid.
11. Randall E. Stross, *Bulls in the China Shop* (New York: Pantheon, 1991).
12. Hang Yashseng, "Web of Interests and Patterns of Behavior of Chinese Local Economic Bureaucracies and Enterprises During Reforms," *The China Quarterly* (September 1990): 431-58.
13. Organization Resources Counselors, Inc., *Multinationals in China: Human Resources Practices and Issues in the PRC* (New York: Rockefeller Center, 1986).
14. Ibid.
15. James A. Wall, Jr., "Managers in the People's Republic of China," *Executive,* 4 May 1994, 19-32.

16. Julia S. Sensenbrenner and John Sensenbrenner, "Personal Priorities: Strategies for Finding and Keeping Good Employees in Shanghai's Competitive Labor Market," *China Business Review* (November-December 1994): 40-45.

For Further Reading

Bian, Yanjie. *Work and Inequality in Urban China.* Albany, New York: State University of New York Press, 1994

Devine, Elizabeth, and Nancy L. Devine. *The Travelers' Guide to Asian Customs and Manners.* New York: St. Martin's Press, 1986

Quangyu, Huang, Richard S. Andrulis, and Chen Tong. *A Guide to Successful Business Relations with the Chinese: Opening the Great Wall's Gate.* Binghamton, New York: Haworth Press, 1994

Schell, Orville. *Mandate of Heaven: A New Generation of Entrepreneurs, Dissidents, Bohemians, and Technocrats Lays Claim to China's Future.* New York: Simon & Scheuster, 1994.

Wenzhong, Hu and Cornelius L. Grove. *Encountering the Chinese: A Guide for Americans.* Yarmouth, Maine: Intercultural Press, 1991.

5

Negotiations

Chinese negotiation strategies and practices are extremely different from those of Europeans and Americans. As a result, many contracts give the Chinese partners unusual advantages. Knowledge of how the Chinese negotiating process works can reduce these inequalities, even though experienced global negotiators see Chinese negotiators as among the world's best and toughest.

A few decades ago, few Chinese were experienced in dealing with foreigners, especially Westerners, and few were familiar with Western languages. As a consequence, a group of professional Chinese negotiators emerged. Foreigners negotiated with these professionals and seldom dealt with their business counterparts. Although this practice has decreased in recent years, negotiation specialists still exist.

These specialists present unique problems. They frequently are not familiar with a specific proposal's technical details and must be carefully taught all facets of a proposed venture. This increases the time needed to complete the preliminary stages of negotiation.

Negotiation specialists offer another challenge. Their goal is to achieve concessions rather than an agreement per se, since they are judged on how many concessions they gain rather than on the number of negotiations they conclude. The ability to show bargaining success may be more important than achieving an agreement, and a failed negotiation can be explained as a refusal to cave in to unreasonable demands. It is important for negotiation specialists to feel that they have won a number of bargaining victories. In this way, they have maintained face.

Chinese Negotiating Logic

Western thinking easily uses abstractions linked to sets of logically connected units. The Chinese mindset, by contrast, emphasizes the concrete and the particular. Words, whether oral or written, express individual, concrete ideas rather than abstract concepts. These differences in thinking and language are reflected in negotiating styles. The Chinese prefer to discuss each issue separately, while Westerners—and Americans in particular—frequently link two or more issues together. They combine related issues into packages, then negotiate each package of issues as a separate unit.

Westerners also rank issues or groups of issues in order of perceived importance. Often, they begin negotiating the most important topics first, and their negotiations become increasingly lax when topics of lesser importance are discussed.

To Chinese negotiators, all issues are equally important, and each issue should receive the same amount of attention, no matter the differences in cost or significance. This makes Americans impatient, and they often yield advantage on lesser issues to save time and to place more important issues on the agenda as soon as possible. The wisest strategy for Western negotiators, however, is to have patience and establish the agenda, if possible.

Americans need to be prepared to discuss each negotiating issue in great detail and to take each issue equally seriously. In addition, agreement on what is seen as a lesser issue does not mean that future negotiations will be easier or that a more cooperative stance is being developed.

Knowing how impatient Americans are, Chinese negotiators may spend inordinate amounts of time on lesser issues in the hope that their opponents will relax their guard. Each negotiating session essentially starts fresh. Yielding on a lesser issue will not make Chinese negotiators more grateful, unless the action is linked to another specific issue. Since each issue is defined as equal to the others, ceding on a minor point merely makes Chinese negotiators eager to gain as much advantage as possible on the next items.

As previously noted, American negotiators like to package related items and negotiate them as a unit to save time. Chinese negotiators do not like this practice. They prefer to deal with one item at a time, even if a package of issues is presented. They will often return to specific items in a package at a later time if each item has not yet been settled.

Further, combining items can often be used by the Chinese to their advantage after a contract has been signed. They may redefine parts of an agreed-on package as ambiguous or in ways that offer them an advantage.

In spite of extensive economic reform and privatization, business in China is still viewed as more than profit for those involved. While many entrepreneurs do seek personal profit, most business deals in China continue to have a national dimension. The Chinese wish to develop economically, in large part because it is beneficial for China and Chinese culture to do so.

When negotiating, projects should be couched in terms of the *social* benefits the projects offer, not just the profit. Provincial and municipal officials, as well as officials in Beijing, will hesitate to welcome foreigners unless they can help China as a whole. Negotiations should contain a concern for the welfare of the local town or province as well as for that of the major parties.

Good Guy-Bad Guy

It is difficult for foreigners to determine who the major decision makers are when negotiating with Chinese. The Chinese, themselves, may be unclear as to who should be included in the search for consensus. Leadership is collective in China, but decisions are made as much through informal networks, or *guanxi* ties, as through formal channels. In addition, the importance of political considerations forces decision makers to seek as many supporters as possible for a project.

The Chinese frequently take advantage of ignorance on the part of foreigners by adopting a good guy-bad guy strategy. In America, this is called the good cop-bad cop tactic.

The Chinese version of this strategy is for a lower-level official to present a harsh, very demanding position, while indicating that no compromises are possible. This stance continues throughout most of a day, or longer. If the Americans seem unwilling to cede conditions, a more senior official arrives "late" to the meeting. He then offers a compromise or more flexible demands. He appears to be the savior and denounces the lesser Chinese official as a misguided bureaucrat.

The "good guy" then suggests concessions by the foreigner on another matter as an exchange. If this does not happen, the foreigner is told he is selfish and uncooperative and that talks may have to stop or at least recess for a week.

During this time, the Americans are living in a hotel with little to do and are forced to report to their superiors that no progress is being made. After a week of this treatment, the Americans may be in a more conciliatory mood when negotiating with the "good guy" on the Chinese negotiating team.

Word Games

Chinese negotiators avoid total bluffs and outright lies. They are capable, however, of claiming that a current demand "violates the spirit" of an earlier agreement. They will express indignation that the Western negotiators suddenly threaten to destroy the harmonious atmosphere and the "friendship" that has been established. Such tactics place American negotiators on the defensive. A similar tactic of Chinese negotiators is to claim that past injustices on the part of the West vis-à-vis China demand that the American negotiators cede to a demand.

Guidelines for U.S. Negotiators

The U.S. Department of State has published the following list of guidelines for U.S. negotiators; some are discussed in greater detail in later sections of this chapter:

- Know the substantive issues cold. Chinese officials are meticulous in their preparations. They will use any indication of ignorance or sloppy preparation against their opposites.
- Master the past negotiating record. Chinese officials use past decisions to their advantage, if possible.
- Know your bottom line. The Chinese drag out negotiations if they sense a final position has not been reached.
- Be patient. Don't expect a quick or easy agreement. The Chinese test the others' resolve. They suspect quick agreements, which are seen as failures on their part.
- Avoid time deadlines. The Chinese use deadlines to their

advantage if they sense that the opposite negotiators must achieve total agreement by a certain time. Use the threat of deadlines and departures sparingly.

- Understand the Chinese meaning of "friendship." The Chinese expect favors from their "friends." Don't fall for Chinese flattery and hospitality and promise more than you can deliver. Resist Chinese efforts to shame you or to play on guilt feelings for alleged errors, past injustices, or historical events.

The Chinese Poker Face

A Chinese negotiator does not show satisfaction or dismay, since either encourages the opponent to push for further advantages or make further demands. Western negotiators are seldom able to gauge how a settlement is viewed. Chinese negotiators also receive proposals without showing much response. There is sometimes no hint of whether a proposal is acceptable or unacceptable. There will be no initial show of approval or disapproval. The process of discovering how each issue is viewed takes time. There are no specific hints as to the degree of acceptability or what agenda items are nonnegotiable.

This "poker face" stance creates a number of difficulties. There is no way at first to determine how responsive Chinese negotiators are to a series of proposals. Each must be discussed in turn until the negotiating process results in some understanding of the Chinese positions. This adds to the time needed for negotiations. This stance also frustrates inexperienced and impatient Western negotiators, who feel that little progress is being made on more vital issues.

The Chinese are also prone to present nonnegotiable issues, usually within an ideological context. That is, they state that socialist ideology does not allow them to consider a specific issue or concession, such as giving the foreign investor the power to choose and dismiss workers. They will also state that a proposal insults the Chinese people and is an example of capitalist greed.

However, more pragmatic concerns remain important, and "nonnegotiable" demands nevertheless retain some flexibility. Often, these issues are quietly dropped out of the discussion and will disappear from the agenda if the foreign negotiator is adamant that such issues are completely irrelevant or nonnegotiable.

Negotiators can also suggest a trade-off between one nonnegotiable issue and another. The Americans might suggest that in view of the "friendship" between the two countries, their company will increase the training period of the joint venture's engineers in exchange for the right to interview all graduating seniors from a high-prestige engineering university who desire interviews.

This demand will have to be negotiated by the Chinese with the officials from the local employment bureau and university, but this type of offer is highly attractive to the Chinese. The extension of those involved in the negotiations, unfortunately, increases the time needed to reach a final decision.

American negotiators need to learn when to forget earlier demands. No one gloats, cheers, or indicates that a compromise has, in fact, been made. The "poker face" should be maintained by both parties.

Time and Frustration

The time element is one of the greatest frustrations experienced by Westerners when negotiating with Chinese, yet it is crucial. Baldly stated, negotiations with Chinese take on the average three to five times longer than do negotiations among Westerners. The impatience Westerners develop during negotiations may cause them to sign contracts that would be unacceptable in other cultural contexts.

Time is money for Westerners, especially for North Americans. A basic assumption of American-style capitalism is that the faster that money or goods change hands, the greater the increase in value and the larger the profits. There is no such assumption in China, except for the relatively few entrepreneurs that exist. Time in China is a lifetime commitment, and no long-term or short-term errors will be made through hasty and hurried decisions. It is not unusual for sales to China to take five years to finalize. Decisions to export to the West may take less time, but not necessarily.

In all probability, several negotiations are going on simultaneously with a foreign company's competitors. Often the same Chinese personnel are negotiating with the competitors. This necessarily takes more time as the Chinese make counteroffers to one group or another. In other instances, two negotiating teams are rotated from one Western competitor to another.

There are many other reasons for an extended period of negotiations. Because they have much longer time horizons than do Westerners, the Chinese seldom feel an urgency to reach agreements. Then, too, decision making is a slower process in China, and decisions have more implications for Chinese managers than for Americans or for Westerners in general.

Chinese bureaucrats feel that it is safer to do nothing than to act rashly. It is always better in China to delay reaching a decision than to make a wrong decision. Therefore, negotiation principals are seldom in a hurry to achieve an agreement. As mentioned earlier, a quick decision may seem to others as indicating that one has given too many concessions.

In addition, negotiations may be used as learning opportunities. Longer negotiations give participants experience in dealing with foreigners or opportunities to learn new technology. Often negotiators bring friends and colleagues with them. The foreigners may not know exactly why these newcomers are present, or what their official capacities are. The best reaction is to accept the visitors and gradually learn why they are in attendance.

Some are present to gain experience in dealing with foreign firms or to practice their English language skills. The newcomers may merely be curious or may wish to observe foreigners for future reference. Or they may be decision makers themselves. Others may simply want to meet foreigners in case *guanxi* relations can be established. Chinese officials may want to meet American negotiators because they wish to send a son or daughter to an American university. They may be seeking information on U.S. universities and their application policies or an American sponsor for a child.

Newcomers are present because they have *guanxi* ties with an official negotiator. Doing a third person a favor may forge a personal link. In this case, be as helpful as possible and treat these visitors as if they were officially designated negotiators.

Some visitors may merely be curious or may want to learn about the latest technology or Western consumer fads. They too define negotiations as learning opportunities. These Chinese are eager to learn about the West and have probably asked a friend to bring them to the negotiation sessions. We recommend two reactions to this situation.

First, accept their presence and participation. They may ask questions that others want answered. These questions provide insight to Chinese interests as well as to areas of ignorance. Accepting the participation of these individuals also indicates courtesy on your part. This creates respect and you gain face. As indicated earlier, allowing their participation creates a debt in your favor with their sponsors. These visitors may also be able to return the favor at a later time. One cannot have too many friends or *guanxi* relationships.

Second, be prepared to present more technical information than usual when negotiating with Chinese. They not only wish to learn but also feel more comfortable with large amounts of technical data. Detailed technical presentations are necessary even though they extend the negotiation time. An outside visitor who demands technical information is actually doing Westerners a favor, since such demands provide opportunities to present more data as well as to determine what other information is needed.

The Chinese do not avoid repetition. If a newcomer—official or otherwise—asks for information that has been presented during earlier sessions, it is best to repeat it, but in a somewhat different way. It may be that a previous presentation was not clearly understood by the official negotiators, and they are too embarrassed to ask for clarification. The newcomer may have been brought in just to ask for a repetition, so that no one will lose face.

In China, students almost never ask questions of their teachers. Doing so indicates either that the student did not understand, and therefore is embarrassed, or that the lecturer was unclear, and therefore he loses face and is also embarrassed. Questions are more easily introduced by third parties. Thus, foreign negotiators should not hesitate to repeat a presentation if a third party requests information already presented. The need may originate from officially interested parties who wish to remain anonymous.

Repetition is also a hallmark of Chinese education; it is the habitual way of learning. Foreign negotiators should always be prepared to repeat presentations, especially those that are technically complex.

Overlapping Responsibilities

A major negotiating consideration is the complexity of the issue. More complex matters are handled by increasing numbers of bureaucracies and bureaucratic levels. A transaction may involve several central government bureaus, one or more municipal divisions, a provincial government, and several agencies.

The Chinese Ministry of Foreign Economic Relations and Trade (MOFERT) is involved in all aspects of foreign trade. Most issues involving foreign trade, especially imports, must obtain MOFERT approval. The China Council for Promotion of International Trade (CCPIT) is theoretically under the jurisdiction of MOFERT but maintains some independence. CCPIT handles most economic disputes involving foreigners, such as contract disagreements. This partial independence from MOFERT forces foreigners to reach agreement with both parties. The jurisdiction of these two groups overlaps slightly, and their respective officials at times have different agendas and aims on the same issue. One agency may have more hard-liners or more liberals as members than the other, so that shifting political winds affect their decisions and interests.

Foreign trade corporations (FTCs) link local and national agencies dealing with foreign groups. There are a number of emerging ministries involved in international trade issues, the most important are listed in Chapter 3. There are also banking agencies that concern themselves with international currency matters.

Bureaucratic responsibilities tend to be vague in China, and directives are seldom clear-cut. They are also overlapping in order to share responsibilities (and blame) and to maintain control. In addition, because of the rapid pace of reforms in recent years, many Chinese officials are unclear about how to implement these reforms, even if they wished to do so.

As a consequence, a large number of interested persons must agree to a contract involving foreigners, although their authority to do so may not be clear. Westerners should not reject anyone who wishes to be included in negotiations. In fact, it may be necessary to "reward" some of these persons in order to get an agreement. How central these outsiders are to achieving an agreement is always difficult to decide. They may have the authority or personal influence (*guanxi*) to determine the ultimate success or failure of negotiations. In summary, a central task of negotiators is deciding who, in fact, has the authority to make major decisions.

Essentially, final decisions will be heavily influenced by persons outside the negotiating team. Foreigners may never completely know the persons involved in a final decision on the Chinese side. This situation demands extreme patience, since your Chinese negotiating counterparts are simultaneously negotiating with officials at all levels as well as with other interested or influential persons. Often, it may be necessary to conspire with the Chinese partners to hammer out a deal that officials will accept.

Large Negotiating Teams

Chinese negotiating teams, as indicated in the previous discussion, are large—usually three or four times the size of their Western counterparts. Since the style of Chinese decision makers is participative, they keep as many colleagues and subordinates informed as possible. All of these people also want to consult with one another. This means more persons have to be convinced, and more time is needed for consultations between sessions.

The membership of these teams also rotates frequently when new persons become interested or involved or a member sends a substitute when personal attendance is not possible. This high rotation level results in even more repetition and demands more time.

The first American response to the costs of sending a negotiating team to China is to send as few persons as possible. However, sending a minimal number indicates to the Chinese that the firm is not serious in its attempts to achieve a contract. An exception to this is when a Western firm sends its highest officials as a symbolic gesture of the importance of the negotiations. Generally, however, a larger-than-usual negotiation team should be sent to China.

Larger teams are useful for another reason. First, as has been discussed, the Chinese expect long and repetitive presentations. Sending a small number results in overwork of the team members. When extensive technical discussions are requested by the Chinese, foreigners need a large team whose members have broad knowledge.

The second response to the costs of sending a negotiating team to China is to hurry negotiations and reach an early decision. This strategy will not work. Few contracts with the Chinese will be signed quickly. The Chinese mindset and bureaucratic conditions in China do not allow for quick decisions. Nor do most Chinese want a quick end to negotiations, for reasons discussed earlier in this chapter.

The only way a quick decision is reached is for the Westerners to concede all advantages and agree to a contract that is completely against their interests. The Chinese will hesitate even under such conditions for fear they made concessions too quickly.

A third response to the high costs of sending negotiating teams to China is try to negotiate as much as possible through fax and other impersonal forms of correspondence. This type of response is almost always counterproductive. Although some groundwork may be prepared through overseas communication, the Chinese will not take great interest in a proposal until personal, face-to-face relationships have been established. The Chinese do not feel comfortable in making decisions through telex or other forms of communication. Achieving any but minimal progress demands at least several visits on the part of the foreign party.

A useful strategy that the Chinese appreciate is for a Western firm to invite a few Chinese officials, at the firm's expense, to visit the facilities in the United States and meet the company officials and representatives. An invited tour of this type may be cheaper than sending company officials to China for preliminary meetings. The rule of thumb is that a quick decision is impossible to achieve without being completely destructive to the Westerner's interest.

Claims of Weakness

The usual Western strategy at the start of negotiations is to appear as strong as possible. The strategy is to intimidate opponents by an early show of force. The Chinese strategy is the opposite—to appear more vulnerable than is the case. Such a position is influenced by the traditional Asian show of humility. Chinese negotiators praise their opponents and stress their own relative weakness and ineptitude.

Expressions of weakness and vulnerability not only present a humble, polite facade, but they also imply that the strong should help the weak. If their claims of weakness are accepted, the Chinese ask for concessions, as due the weak from the strong.

Westerners can also use this "poor orphan" play. They should answer requests for concessions with claims that their company finances are too weak, that currency exchange problems exist, and similar excuses. Continue throughout negotiations to apologize for your firm's small size, international inexperience, or whatever deficiencies may exist, in fact or in fancy. The Chinese are doing the same.

This humble position is not a comfortable tactic for the Western, especially for the American, self-image. But it disarms the Chinese negotiators' own claims of weaknesses. Remember that the Chinese are sophisticated enough to thoroughly investigate a company before they meet with its representatives. The Chinese will know which claims of weaknesses are valid and which ones are mere form. On the other hand, Chinese negotiators will also be familiar with their opponents' strengths. Bluffs of exaggerated strengths are quickly exposed.

Weaknesses often have to be seen by the Chinese to be believed. Newcomers to China tend to live in first-class hotels and to enjoy sumptuous banquets and other amenities. While the comfort of expatriates is a major consideration, Westerners are also trying to establish their image. Most Westerners stay in international-class hotels that would be far too expensive for the Chinese negotiators. Claims of being "poor orphans" should be supported by less extravagant living arrangements and expenses.

Western representatives can also claim that the budget does not allow for numerous gifts or product samples unless the representatives live more simply than usual. They can claim that costs preclude them from making trans-Pacific calls to comply with certain Chinese requests for immediate technical information.

First Offers

The usual Western strategy for first offers is to expect to compromise. Negotiation is seen as the process of giving advantages to the other party in exchange for concessions. Western negotiators customarily present unrealistically high or low first offers, then gradually make concessions until the parties reach an acceptable meeting point. In China, however, the best strategy is to make the first offer fairly close to the most acceptable final offer. That is, the first offer should be only 10 or 20 percent away from the final offer.

After both parties have made their first offers, negotiators attempt to wear down opponents through fatigue, boredom, impatience, and a lack of time. The Chinese strategy is to slow the pace of negotiation so that Western opponents become impatient and make concessions in the hopes the other party will also offer compromises.

The Western strategy of presenting unreasonable first offers is misguided when dealing with Chinese. The Chinese accept a concession and then patiently wait for another. Westerners should state their position and concede as little as possible afterwards. Otherwise, the last stages of negotiation will consist of a series of small concessions on the part of the foreigner until the agreement has little hope of becoming profitable.

When Chinese negotiators expect to lose on an issue, they may offer a new, completely unrelated proposal or demand. They have not agreed to the first proposal, but have merely avoided making a decision by going to another issue. Westerners, faced with a sudden change of issues, are likely to assume that agreement on the first issue has been reached, which is not true. What has happened is a change of attention. The Chinese will return to the first issue when conditions seem more favorable.

Delay Tactics

The use of delay tactics is common among Chinese negotiators. The worst foreign response to these delays is to demand a speed up in negotiations or to threaten that unless some progress is made the

American team will end discussions and go home. These reactions cause Westerners to lose face and are seen as signs of weakness. The Chinese negotiators expect the Westerner to offer some minor (or major) concession as a sign of goodwill. But they will not be motivated to offer a concession in exchange. They have just gained a minor victory and will now push for others.

Three strategies are effective in response to delay behavior. The first and best is to provide your own delay. That is, meet obstinacy with your own stalling. Slow down the pace of negotiation and refuse to budge from your original position. This policy is psychologically difficult for Americans, since they are used to a faster negotiation pace and because the negotiators want to return home as soon as possible. It is also difficult to explain the lack of progress and the high costs of negotiating to superiors at the home office. Remember that a concession at this time will not be seen as an offer for mutual compromises. Giving in to stall tactics merely signifies your weakness.

A second response to delay tactics is to ask a third party to mediate. Third party mediators can often suggest the real cause for delay. To bring in a third party, American negotiators must have established a wide network of *guanxi* relationships with officials not directly involved in the negotiation. A series of meetings with provincial and municipal officials might result in pressures to advance negotiation. For example, an offer to deposit foreign currency in a local bank might cause bank officials to seek out the Chinese negotiators and "suggest" a faster pace of negotiation.

The third response to stalling is to determine whether the delays are real or symbolic. It may be that obstinacy is caused by a desire to save face or to look tough to colleagues and superiors. It may be that the Chinese negotiators wish to appear unyielding to a superior or outside official not directly involved in the negotiation. A visit to such authority figures might end the negotiation blockage.

If the delay is symbolic, some symbolic concessions may be necessary. A negotiator may offer a minor concession that costs relatively little but reflects well on the Chinese negotiator, such as an offer to train ten engineers at the main plant rather than five, which would probably be necessary eventually. Or a "deal" can be made so that each party retreats a little from a previous position, but each can show a negotiating victory. The foreign investor can offer to build the *danwei* a hospital in exchange for the right to interview—and reject if necessary—job applicants.

Sometimes minor concessions are useful, although they may or may not gain an advantage. The Chinese may consider a symbolic concession the result of their superior negotiating tactics, while they continue to define the Westerners as weak. So a symbolic concession may only invite additional unilateral demands and delay tactics. Another useful response is to indicate the need for time to discuss matters with colleagues and the home office, and to request a break in the sessions. A recess may result in an end to delay tactics.

The "Tit-for-tat" Strategy

Unilateral demands and delay tactics on the part of Chinese negotiators may also be met by a "tit-for-tat" or "yes-but" response. This response announces a concession but at the same time demands a concession from the opposite members. The "tit-for-tat" strategy allows the Chinese negotiators to save face and show superiors that they have gained a victory, even if it is symbolic. On the Western side, the negotiators have indicated that a concession must be met by a similar concession, in a fair exchange. This strategy indicates a willingness to compromise without showing weakness.

If the demand is understood as largely symbolic, the "tit-for-tat" response equalizes the costs of concession. The Western negotiator may accept the demand that more resources be spent training Chinese managers (who might become competitors in the future) *if* the Chinese are willing to reduce the land rental fees for a proposed factory.

It is always best to link a concession to a demand. Otherwise, negotiations develop into a series of demands for unilateral concessions. The "tit-for-tat" strategy also indicates that further demands for concession will be met by corresponding and immediate demands in turn. Thus the Americans appear resolute and conciliatory at the same time.

Discovering the Negotiators

Chinese negotiators are usually representatives rather than decision makers. At the very least, they will consult with colleagues, superiors, *guanxi* partners, and shadow government and Communist Party officials. Chinese negotiators generally spend as much time or more negotiating the same issue with other Chinese as with Westerners. It is best, though often difficult, to determine all unofficially and officially interested parties.

This search takes time, but it saves effort in the long run. Recognizing the involved parties allows foreign negotiators to determine what is really required to conclude an agreement. Proposals always involve many self-interests, some of which may not be openly discussed.

A provincial official might accept a proposal only if the foreign partner offers free training of personnel or a promise to buy materials only locally. This official may also be worried that a proposed factory might make too much demand on the province's limited electric power resources. He might encourage the acceptance of a venture if the foreign partner agrees to import a power plant that will meet the needs of the new factory and serve the community as well.

The foreign negotiator, knowing this preference, might volunteer that the company will provide and install a power source for the proposed factory if the Chinese partners reduce their charges for leasing land and building the factory. The Chinese can then sell the excess energy at a discount to other interested and potentially powerful associates. The negotiator thereby makes the provincial official an ally and links the compromise to a reduced cost in another area. Thus, at no additional cost, the Westerner gains a valuable ally.

Keeping Notes

Careful notes should be kept of all meetings. The Chinese will do the same and will take advantage of the Western negotiators if they indicate any ignorance of past activities. After each meeting, these notes should be the basis of a memorandum that is sent to the Chinese officials. Cross-cultural communication is ambiguous and error-prone at best. It is easy to misunderstand a nod or a spoken "yes." In Asian cultures, a "yes" may mean "maybe," "I'm listening," "no," or even "yes." But the last should never be assumed.

In addition, a Chinese negotiator may be told later by higher-level officials that "yes" was wrong and should be retracted if possible. A written memorandum or *aide-m'emoire,* signed by both parties, establishes official recognition and makes unilateral last-minute changes less likely.

The Chinese will probably try to leave "gray areas" in a formal agreement. Vague clauses frequently become future points of negotiation and disagreement. Whenever it is to their advantage, the

Chinese will point to vagueness in an agreement and insist that their interpretations are the ones already agreed upon. They are also quite willing to resume extended negotiations to gain further advantages.

Detailed memoranda signed by all parties avoid some of these problems. This precludes the Chinese option to "forget" what has been said by not writing it down. The Chinese are willing to reconstruct a past conversation to their advantage if nothing has been written and certified.

Developing Contracts

Contracts with Chinese partners should be as detailed as possible and should never assume anything or take anything for granted. For example, in one Chinese-American joint venture the American partners agreed to pay for and import workers' uniforms. The provincial government then decreed that these uniforms could be worn outside of the workplace and therefore should be taxed as ordinary clothing. The foreign partner, of course, was expected to pay the tax. Extended renegotiations had to begin after the foreign partner had invested substantial capital in the venture. The foreign partner was at an obvious negotiating disadvantage over a relatively unimportant item. Ceding many such issues, however, can destroy the chances for profit.

Contracts with Chinese partners should be extremely detailed and clear. Foreign partners should also expect that contracts will be continuously renegotiated. The Chinese view is that contracts apply only to current circumstances, and therefore a contractual clause becomes invalid if events change the clause's context. Chinese government officials, for example, have rejected a number of contractual promises with foreigners when circumstances changed. When Beijing officials decided that too much foreign currency was being exported by foreign joint-venture partners, the Chinese central banks stopped exchanging local currency into foreign, exportable currencies. This immediately reduced the profits of foreign partners, and the issue had to be renegotiated.

Additional Guidelines for U.S. Negotiators

The U.S. Department of State suggests the following additional guidelines for negotiating with the Chinese:
- Never lose your temper, or show anger.
- Be ready to end negotiations if a good deal is impossible. Do

not be tied to a policy of entering China at any cost.

- Indicate a long-term interest in doing business in China.
- Be ready to compromise and expect compromise in exchange.
- Prepare the Chinese for new information. The Chinese do not like to be surprised.
- Repeat often. Languages and cultural problems always exist.
- Never ad lib or talk "off the record." The Chinese take note of *everything* said during negotiations and elsewhere.

The Place of Lawyers

As mentioned in earlier chapters, the Chinese legal system is constantly changing, and it has traditionally been used to keep events from happening or to control persons. Historically, the law has been manipulated by the powerful to control the weak as well as to gain personal advantage. Consequently, the law is mistrusted in China, and the Chinese prefer to establish personal relationships rather than legal ones. Legal issues should be addressed during the later stages of a negotiation. In addition, lawyers should be brought into the negotiations only in the last stages, after general principles and personal trust have been established.

American Negotiating Strengths

Americans, and Westerners in general, have several positions of strength when negotiating with the Chinese. The major strength is American technology and technological expertise, which the Chinese are eager to import. In fact, they are willing to acquire prestigious state-of-the-art technology even if it is not cost-effective within a Chinese context. The Chinese wish to catch up with the West, regardless of the costs.

A proposal is more likely to be accepted if it includes an offer to transfer the latest technology into China. If, during negotiations, the Chinese demand a larger capital investment, a useful counteroffer is a smaller initial investment and more state-of-the-art machinery.

Another area of American superiority is technical and administrative expertise. The Chinese wish to absorb Western technological and managerial abilities as fast as possible. This desire is a major reason Westerners are allowed into China in the first place. Offers to train or educate Chinese personnel are extremely welcome and, in fact, are usually demanded as part of any agreement. Whenever an impasse occurs during negotiations, an offer to absorb the costs of training workers or managers in exchange for an advantage elsewhere in the agreement will be received positively.

For example, a Chinese demand that housing for expatriate workers be paid for by the foreign partner could be countered by an offer to pay for 100 hours of classroom training for all new workers in exchange for the Chinese partners' providing all housing and utilities for foreign workers. The Chinese costs for these services are low, since they do not involve the expenditure of foreign currency, but importing teachers would entail five to ten times the housing costs.

Clauses that include training attract the support of both government officials and prospective local partners. The ability to train personnel at all levels is a major negotiating advantage enjoyed by Americans.

In addition to offering to train local personnel, the training advantage can be used in several other ways. One strategy is to offer to train a limited number of personnel in the United States. Although expensive, this offer is extremely attractive to the Chinese, and the training costs can be offset by negotiated savings in other areas. For example, a foreign negotiator may offer to train a selected number of Chinese managers and supervisors in America if the Chinese reduce local taxes or building and remodeling costs by an equivalent amount. The result is that local costs are reduced in exchange for a better-trained labor force. All partners gain an advantage.

The offer to train workers in China or in the United States also provides a diplomatic way to reject exorbitant demands. A response to an unacceptable demand is to accept a small part of the demand in exchange for a ten-week training program for five managers to take place in the United States. A useful "yes-but" response of Americans is to yield to a Chinese demand in exchange for a *decrease* in training.

Another appreciated gift or negotiating point on the part of Americans is to sponsor a number of scholarships to U.S. universities, though this may be seen as bribery by many. Counterproposals can include an offer to provide five or ten scholarships for the children of the most qualified workers. More welcome, but less ethical, is to offer the head of a Chinese delegation a number of scholarships that the official can distribute at will. This allows the Chinese partner to offer scholarships to government officials whose support is needed. The possibility of transferring knowledge in any form is a very strong negotiating card held by foreigners in general and by Americans in particular.

Another strength of American negotiators is the ability to end negotiations and return home. This strategy is often ignored by Americans, who become obsessed with reaching an agreement. However, stopping negotiations must be linked to willingness to be flexible and patient.

It is better not to threaten that negotiations will cease if a solution is not found by a certain time. The Chinese do not respond well to threats, and they may also assume the threats are bluffs. More effective is to declare an impasse "difficult" and that a temporary recess is in order.

For example, an impasse will often occur as the Chinese make unilateral demands and refuse to consider compromises. One response might be to suggest a recess, then try to discover—through third parties, personal relationships, and other avenues—why the impasse exists. If no answer is found, it is proper to declare that since no progress is being made, the negotiating team will return home for a while. The Americans then should pack their belongings and fly home. The costs of the return overseas flights will most likely be less than the direct and indirect costs of staying in China until the impasse ends.

Leaving is a useful tactic because the Chinese hosts may be unwilling to declare openly that a rejected agreement cannot or will not ever be achieved. Declaring a recess allows both parties to save face, even though a contract is totally rejected. Once home, the foreign negotiating team can exchange messages and ask third parties for advice. If the project has really been rejected, the negotiations essentially die a slow death, and no one is personally embarrassed by their demise.

Another related strategy is for the Americans to declare a time limit for the negotiations, though this is not a preferred tactic for several reasons. First, as has been noted previously, Americans tend to underestimate the time needed to achieve a major decision in China. The Chinese negotiators may be eager to arrive at a mutually beneficial agreement, but it may be impossible to reach agreement using an American time-scale. Establishing a time limit is best done after negotiations have begun and the negotiators have some idea of the probable rate of progress.

Second, the Chinese may use a time limit to their advantage. If they sense the Americans are more eager than they are to conclude an agreement, the Chinese negotiators may stall to see if the Americans become nervous as the time limit approaches. The Americans may then become trapped by their own strategy and make too many compromises at the last minute.

Since the Chinese may also be negotiating with competing foreign companies, they are willing to test one firm against the other. This slows the pace of negotiations even more.

If a departure date is postponed, and the parties have not reached an agreement, then the Chinese have won a victory and will continue to delay and stall. They have lost nothing, and the credibility of the Americans has been destroyed.

Controlling the Agenda

Since most negotiations take place in China, Chinese officials have a home court advantage. Before negotiations in China begin, it is wise to draft an agenda to ensure that the issues most important to the Westerners, such as currency matters, credit, import/export restrictions, and labor matters, are discussed first.

Westerners often begin agreements on minor issues with the assumption that this creates a snowball effect and makes other agreements more likely. This is a false assumption. When dealing with Chinese representatives, it is better to agree on core issues first. As mentioned earlier, each issue is equally important to the Chinese, and minor questions take the same amount of time to resolve as major ones. The Chinese will delay on minor issues in the expectation the foreign guests will become impatient and then concede more easily on major matters.

It is not always possible to control an agenda, though announcing a time limit for negotiation is a way to do so. Even with an agenda, the Americans must be prepared to temporarily leave an issue and turn their attention to another item if progress stalls or the time limit set for an item has been reached.

Americans will want to discuss items in a linear fashion: one issue is taken up, discussion continues until an agreement is reached, then a new issue is taken up. The Chinese, by contrast, will skip from one issue to another before a conclusion on the first has been reached. They enjoy doing so if they sense this places them at a psychological advantage. Because they always take good notes of the proceedings, it is easy for them to resume a previous conversation.

Team Members

Negotiating teams should be fairly large by Western standards. The members should be compatible and able to work together, since negotiations with Chinese can take years. At least one or two members should be fluent in Chinese. This keeps the Chinese negotiators from talking among themselves.

In addition, the U.S. team should have its own translators. It is dangerous to use the opponents' translators, and temporarily hired translators may not be loyal to American interests. Translators are best hired in Hong Kong rather than in Beijing, if there are no other alternatives.

Having Mandarin speakers as permanent members of the team ensures their loyalty. They are also available to offer personal insights as to the emotional shading and content of verbal exchanges. In the Chinese culture, gestures, tones of voice, and other aspects of body language and verbal expressions denote meaning. These nuances are almost impossible for translators to pass on to others during a session. They are also easily forgotten, and should be discussed and written down as soon as possible. For example, an "it is possible," might be translated "this probably means no," based on the tone or body language of the speaker. Debriefing sessions soon after negotiation periods are very important when dealing with Chinese negotiators.

A large negotiation team offers another advantage. Larger teams make possible a greater variety of talents and specialties among members. One member, for example, should be a specialist in Chinese law. Chinese negotiators do not assume responsibility for educating foreigners on a legal system that is ambiguous and constantly changing in content and interpretation. Foreigners who fail to take advantage of the legal system are on their own.

After a Contract Is Signed

The Chinese enjoy the reputation of scrupulously following the conditions of a contract. The consensus, participative form of decision making in China ensures that once a project is accepted, all involved and interested parties have had input and therefore support is universal. The fact that all contractual conditions will be followed to the letter demands that a contract be comprehensive in the first place.

However, the Chinese assume that a contract is valid only as long as the original conditions are maintained. If circumstances change after signing a contract, then the contract needs to be changed to fit a new reality. This means that some members of the original negotiating team should be retained as future negotiators for as long as the project lasts. These experienced negotiators can renegotiate without requiring extensive background briefings They will also have developed the personal relationships with Chinese colleagues that are so important.

According to the American mindset, once a contract has been negotiated, any change entails a lawsuit for breach of contract. The Asian mindset, however, is that contracts are evolving documents for the benefit of all parties and should be renegotiated when conditions change.

Those having concluded a contract with the Chinese should be flexible enough to consider contractual changes whenever requested. These renegotiations can be advantageous, if the Chinese feel that the eventual exchanges will be are mutually beneficial.

On the other hand, complex contracts necessarily contain "gray areas" that will need renegotiation over a period of time, yet another reason for maintaining an experienced negotiating team to handle these issues as they emerge. While the Chinese will conform to their contractual responsibilities, gray areas are fair game for advantageous interpretations.

A final issue exists after negotiations have been completed: Government agencies at all levels are likely to add charges and new "taxes" as the need arises. These are not the fault of the Chinese partners, and they should not be blamed for these increased costs. Government officials frequently and arbitrarily increase taxes and fees or invent new levies of one type or another, partly to see if such attempts will succeed. These new charges must be negotiated with the Chinese officials, and the Chinese partners can greatly help in these matters.

Foreigners in China face other unexpected financial demands. Before the 1989 Tiananmen Square events, when hotel and office spaces were at a premium, hotel management would try to add nonnegotiated fees and increased charges at irregular intervals. Suddenly, foreign companies would be unilaterally charged for a "residency use" or for the "commercial use" of a suite. From 1980 to 1989, when housing resources for foreigners were limited, hotels frequently increased rentals by increasing previously nonexistent fees. Hotels also added charges for services that had been included in previous rentals or for services not used, such as maid service or doorman fees.

It is usually impossible to completely resist such demands, since vacant hotel and office space is becoming once again scarce. An experienced, full-time representative is needed to withstand these unilateral increases and to negotiate cutbacks. These negotiations have not generally been successful when housing is in short supply, since foreigners have relatively few alternatives. Experienced personnel who have well-established networks can sometimes negotiate these increases in an indirect manner. For example, the mayor of Shanghai at this time is pro-business and pro-foreign business. A foreign firm whose factory rental has been doubled or whose hotel fees have been arbitrarily increased can send its representative to talk to someone in the mayor's office to mediate renegotiation.

For Further Reading

Binnendijk, Hans. *National Negotiating Styles.* Washington, DC: U.S. Department of State, Foreign Service Institute, 1987.

Engholm, Christopher. *When Business East Meets Business West.* New York: Wiley, 1991.

Eiteman, David K. "American Executives' Perceptions of Negotiating Joint Ventures with the People's Republic of China: Lessons Learned." *Columbia Journal of World Business* 25 (Winter): 59-25.

Moran, Robert T. and William G. Stripp. *Dynamics Of Successful International Business Negotiations.* Houston, Texas: Gulf Publishing, 1991.

Seligman, Scott D. *Dealing With the Chinese.* New York: Warner Books, 1989.

6

Social and
Business Etiquette

The Communist regime reacted strongly against the excesses of the wealthy of the previous dynasties and governments. There were strenuous efforts to end luxurious lifestyles and what were defined as decadent and immoral behaviors, such as the use of narcotic drugs and prostitution. The regime promoted and achieved a strict standard of living for the population.

The result is a population not used to more liberal Western standards of morality. When American Motors wanted to impress their Chinese partners after concluding a joint venture to assemble jeeps, American Motors executives invited their Chinese counterparts to a celebration in Las Vegas. The near-nudity and extravagance of the show repelled the Chinese executives, and the agreement was almost canceled. The Chinese are becoming aware of foreign behavior and fashion, and dress in Hong Kong is as stylish as in any European capital. However, mainland Chinese still wear extremely conservative clothing, although the once-prevalent Mao jacket is seldom seen. Visiting foreigners should also wear sedate clothing fashions. For men, dark colors are the norm, though a suit and tie need not be worn continuously or during normal business activities. Women should not expose too much of their bodies.

In the same manner, deportment should be calm and quiet. Individuals lose face when they lose their tempers and speak loudly. Exuberant gestures are to be avoided. People are more likely to be respected when they appear calm and in control of their emotions. Nor do the Chinese react positively to threats and ultimatums.

We stress that those going to China for more than a few days must be patient in the extreme and remain calm at all times. Highstrung, type-A individuals will not achieve much success in China or with the Chinese. A foreigner must adapt to the Chinese pace of business and not become irritated or ruffled, even when provoked (see Exhibit 6-1).

Expressing Anger

Showing anger is a major social error as well as bad strategy. However, there are times when expressing extreme feelings are appropriate and even useful. As we have noted previously, many Chinese do not perceive the need to work hard or to take responsibility. After all, it is usually safer to not do something than to act, since action is more likely to be punished than inaction.

The following story clearly illustrates the problem Americans frequently have with the Chinese. An American working in Changsha, the capital of Hunan, was attempting to evacuate himself and his family during the 1989 Tiananmen Square events, but could not obtain plane tickets to Shanghai, Hong Kong, and then to the United States. Hoping to speed matters along, he composed a telex message to the company office in the United States, containing a list of

---

Exhibit 6-1. What Chinese Do Not Like About Americans

Arrogant	Too rich
Hypocritical	Not friendly
Bossy	Feel superior
Often interrupt	Are not humble or reserved
Complain about Chinese conditions	Laugh at one's attempts to speak English
Not personal; all business	Don't understand the exchange of gifts

Source: Survey of Chinese students at an American University.

telephone numbers and names of persons who he thought would be more accessible and cooperative in issuing appropriate ticket reservations. Later that day, hoping to receive a response from his American superior, he learned that the message had not been sent because the telex clerk was home ill. The other clerks were reading newspapers or napping.

The American lost his temper and created an uproar by demanding that his message be sent immediately and stating that he would not leave or be quiet until the message was sent. The president of his Chinese organization rushed over, made his personal telephone available to the American, and the telex was sent within the hour.

It is sometimes acceptable to indicate one's anger while in China, since not doing so may be seen as hypocritical. Expressions do convey messages to Chinese, and often these displays of emotions are useful. Displays of anger threaten the face of all those concerned, and motivate someone to seek to a solution; however, it is better to indicate feelings quietly rather than to explode into a violent temper tantrum.

If the Chinese feel they are at fault over an issue, then a display or expression of anger and disappointment can produce positive results. Anger should be used very sparingly, however, and should not personally insult individuals, such as calling them lazy fools or inept. Sometimes the reason for anger is beyond the control of anyone present. Often, delays are caused by overlapping bureaucracies, language barriers, and a simple lack of resources. In addition, the frustrations that foreigners feel while in China often reflect petty attitudes and discomforts. Expressing anger over minor issues is inappropriate.

Time and Communications

Foreign corporate representatives in China need considerable responsibility and authority. Beijing's time zone is eight hours later than Greenwich Mean Time and thirteen hours later than U.S. Eastern Standard Time. These differences cause problems in communication, since, generally, the workday is ending in China and beginning in the United States.

Problems are minimized when foreigners in China do not have to continuously contact their home offices. The best employees to send to China on assignments are those who feel comfortable with extensive independence. Those who cannot or will not become autonomous will not do well in China. Working conditions are so different there that home office superiors can seldom second-guess their representatives in China or micro-manage affairs across the Pacific.

International communications are seldom a problem in Beijing, Shanghai, or other large urban centers. Hotels catering to international travelers maintain adequate communication facilities for contact outside China. Telephone connections may take some time to establish, but are generally completed easily. Fax, telex, and other services are available in international hotels and many Friendship Stores. While English operators are usually available, it is sometimes prudent to employ a native speaker to use telex, fax, and telephone facilities. The Chinese postal system is highly efficient and dependable. Mail to and from the United States generally takes from four to ten days and is reliable.

There are eight general major holidays of varying importance: March 8 (International Working Women's Day); May 1 (Labor Day); May 4 (Children's Day); October 1 (National Day); January 1 (New Year's); three days at the end of January and start of February (Chinese New Year); June 1 (Founding of the Chinese Communist Party); August 1 (People's Liberation Army Day); October 1 (National Day).

The Chinese New Year is a lunar holiday and its dates change. It is better not to travel to China just before or after these dates, since many persons take extra leave at that time. Much celebrating occurs during these holidays, with gift exchanges and social visits that include drinking; not much work is completed.

Making Initial Contacts

Making initial contacts is difficult, though there are a number of ways to do so. Attending Chinese trade fairs is one approach, especially if the foreigner wishes to buy goods made in China for export to the West. The Chinese are also beginning to attend trade fairs outside of China, and representatives can be met during such events. There are also Chinese trade missions that travel to various countries to introduce their goods and inspect possible imports into China.

A number of trade and investment organizations, such as the US-China Business Council, can provide initial introductions and information on trade possibilities (see Appendix for addresses). Large banking, accounting, and legal firms have contacts in China, and they offer a full range of China-based services.

Eventually, most attempts to initiate business relations in China involve an agent or representative. This may be a consultant or a potential partner. As the first qualification, such a person must have extensive contacts with Chinese officials and be familiar with local conditions.

Agents in Hong Kong and in Western capitals may have limited experience in a specific areas of China, and their personal contacts may not be extensive. The best representatives are those who are familiar with local business conditions, which can change very quickly in China. U.S. companies need representatives who reside in China to handle day-to-day issues as they occur.

Much business behavior in China occurs behind the scenes. It is important that agents and major employees have or develop considerable local knowledge and personal contacts. The legal system is ambiguous, policies are applied unequally, and they are likely to change rapidly without public announcement. While highly experienced China hands are relatively scarce, it is worth taking the time to develop local expertise on a long-term basis. Often, Chinese joint-venture partners can mediate between foreigners and government and other officials.

At the very least, some company representatives should be given foreign assignments that last for three to five years. These employees need at least a year to develop the Chinese contacts and experiences that make them effective. A core of long-term employees provides stability for those whose stay in China is shorter. These more experienced employees allow short-term and less experienced transients to come and go without a significant loss of efficiency.

Shaking Hands

The first contact with Chinese counterparts is shaking hands, and meaningful impressions are made through handshaking styles. Americans are known throughout Asia by what is generally considered their obnoxious handshakes. Asians, including Chinese, do not use forceful, physical handshakes. The custom is for a handshake to be soft ("fishy" to Westerners) and short. The pumping action is gentle and brief.

Americans are taught to offer handshakes with crushing grips and hard pumping actions. These denote masculine vigor, enthusiasm, and positive greetings. The Chinese define such handshakes as aggressive and unnecessarily violent. Most Westerners and North

Americans wishing to make a positive first expression are advised to tone down their handshakes.

Bowing, Touching, and Body Language

Although most Westerners assume that all Orientals bow when greeting each other, the Chinese do not bow. A slight nod when shaking hands or being introduced is enough body language.

Chinese culture is not a touching culture, in contrast to the Latin and Mediterranean cultures. People do not touch or tap each other when greeting each other or when talking together (see Exhibit 6-2). The American and Latin habit of draping an arm around someone's shoulder to show friendship and agreement is not acceptable in China. Nor should there be any taps on the shoulder when emphasizing a point. Physical contact, except for handshaking, is best avoided when dealing with Chinese.

An exception to the lack of physical contact is found when an honored guest is being conducted somewhere. The host or other official standing next to a foreign guest might gently hold on to the guest's sleeve as a guide or for protection. A Chinese host is likely to hold on to a cuff or sleeve material of a guest when both are climbing or descending stairs or crossing a street. Such contact merely indicates solicitous concern for a guest.

Body language in general should be sedate and controlled. A Westerner loses face when fists are pounded on a table to emphasize a point or to indicate determination. The Chinese view such

---

Exhibit 6-2. Actions to Avoid

- Never touch, poke, backslap, or point.

- Do not summon someone with an upraised, waving finger. Hold your hand out palm down and move your fingers downward. Finger snapping is bad form and insulting.

- Never compliment a female colleague or wife about her looks or dress. Do so indirectly, such as "your child is very pretty, like her mother." Complimenting a child is expected.

- Avoid being informal and egalitarian. Show the leading guest formal courtesy and respect.

- Casual discussion of sex should be avoided.

- Do not talk too much

---

behavior as indicating a loss of control. Self-control, no matter the provocation, is a Confucian ideal that is central to the modern-day Chinese. Equanimity is a sign of culture and superiority.

Body language should also be formal. A visitor should not lean or slouch. Correct posture demands sitting straight and still, or standing without pacing or showing impatience. The listener leans slightly toward a speaker and maintains eye contact to indicate attention and respect.

Smiles are body gestures that have many meanings in Chinese culture. A smile can denote satisfaction and happiness. But a smile at times can also indicate embarrassment and anger. Nor can a smile always be interpreted as agreement. Calm, serene demeanor demands self-control, and a smile may merely be a gesture showing calm and courtesy. Westerners should not always interpret Chinese smiles in a positive manner.

Like a smile, laughter does not always indicate happiness. At times, strained laughter is used when a listener does not want to answer a question. A short laugh instead of a response to a question indicates that either the question is inappropriate or that the answer would be embarrassing for one of the parties. In such circumstances, drop the topic and return to it later in a more roundabout fashion, if the information is vital.

Business Cards

Business cards using Chinese script are necessary identification. The cards should be bilingual, with English on one side and Chinese on the other and should contain as much information as possible. Chinese business cards typically contain more information about the owners than do those from the United States. Multiple ranks or positions should be mentioned if appropriate. Graduate degrees can also be included, since the Chinese respect education.

The Chinese-language side should indicate how a foreign name should be pronounced as well as the rank of the donor, so that appropriate titles can be used. The Chinese wish to know how each person they meet fits into society in relation to themselves, in order to offer proper respect.

Cards are best printed in China, although reliable printers can also be found in Hong Kong and the United States. The written language is somewhat different in Taiwan, because the Chinese Communists have simplified a number of commonly used ideograms, and it is important to use the more modern forms and spellings used in mainland China rather than those used in Taiwan. When ordering business cards outside mainland China, one should state clearly that the cards will not be used in Hong Kong or anywhere outside mainland China proper.

Ideally, bilingual business cards in both Chinese script and English should be available for distribution before leaving for China, since it is best to include them with early correspondence. Again, printers living outside of China *must* be told that the cards will be given to mainland Chinese. Everyone written to should receive a card during the first contact. Cards with Chinese script on one side indicate both a respect for China's customs and an interest in doing long-term business in China. They also help those who are not familiar with European script.

Cards should be exchanged with everyone during introductions to one's Chinese hosts, and no one in the group should be slighted. The Chinese keep these cards in special files for future reference. A person has not been properly introduced until business cards have been exchanged.

Foreigners as Models

The Chinese feelings toward foreigners are ambivalent but respectful. Foreigners serve as models, especially after stable relationships have been established. Foreigners must lead by example whenever possible, since Chinese workers compare behavior against words and note any inconsistencies. If, for example, foreign managers feel that office desks are not kept clean enough, they should clean their own desks and keep them neat. They might also personally clear public areas, such as conference tables, to show how important cleanliness is. Soon, subordinates and others will keep all desks and work surfaces clean and clutter-free.

Since social equality is still a major ideal in contemporary China, foreign managers and executives should demand as few perks as possible. Eating with workers and colleagues in their cafeteria is one way of showing solidarity. Foreign presidents of joint ventures should work full days and not leave work early, even if this means they will face heavy traffic going home. Because the topology of Beijing is flat, the most common means of transportation is the bicycle. A foreigner who arrives at work on a bicycle will be better-liked.

The Chinese are aware that foreigners receive very high salaries and enjoy standards of living few Chinese are able to achieve. It is best not to flaunt this wealth in public and to live as simply as possible.

Language Abilities

Most foreigners dealing with Chinese do not speak Chinese, either Mandarin or local dialects. Mandarin is an especially difficult language for Westerners, since it uses tones to convey meaning. Words may have as many as four meanings, according to the tone used. As a word is spoken, inflection may go up, may go down, may go down then up, and so forth. The word *ma*, for example, may mean "horse" or "mother," according to tone. Cantonese contains six tones, and even Mandarin speakers find Cantonese difficult to understand.

Nevertheless, for those working in Beijing, some familiarity with Mandarin can smooth social interactions. At the very least, the fact that a foreigner is learning Mandarin indicates respect for Chinese culture. The Chinese appreciate efforts foreigners make when trying to say a few words of greetings. For those planning a long-term stay in China, developing a familiarity with spoken Chinese is an excellent strategy. It will also make living in China somewhat easier.

Apologizing

The quickest way to lose face with Chinese is to refuse to apologize. Apologies are expected, even when you are innocent. Any involvement in an embarrassing situation—even if you're blameless—calls for an apology, indicating that you deplore the situation. An apology is not an admission of guilt; it indicates that you recognize that the situation makes you as well as others uncomfortable. By the same token, someone who refuses to apologize is seen as arrogant and uncooperative.

The foreigner should also take apologies with a grain of skepticism. An apology does not include the implicit promise to correct an error, change one's behavior, or make a wrong right. An apology reflects the tension Chinese feel when faced with overt conflict.

In traditional China, people who inconvenienced officials or exposed their crimes were likely to suffer, even when they were innocent. A major responsibility of an official was to keep the peace and maintain order. He was likely to be blamed when someone registered a complaint or threatened the status quo. Someone who disturbed the peace, even if right, angered officials and suffered for this assumed arrogance. The issue is not innocence or guilt, but whether social calm has been maintained or disturbed.

After offering an apology, it is possible to later present your case, if that can be done calmly and without a show of emotions. Better yet, a complaint can be presented by a third party. Apologies do not mean that an issue has been settled, but merely that all parties wish to maintain a surface harmony.

Americans frequently define apologies as signs of either weakness or guilt. In Chinese culture, apologies are merely good manners and a strategy to encourage calmness. In fact, it is possible to receive extra attention if one begins a request with an apology. The Chinese wish to be gracious hosts, but they resist being forced to accede to what may be seen as unreasonable demands. An apology for asking a special favor is more likely to lead to special attention. This is especially true if the Westerner is willing to wait until the request has been debated behind the scenes.

Giving Advice

Their Confucian code of courtesy forces the Chinese to be humble and ask Westerners for advice. The Chinese often express their own and their country's shortcomings. They frequently ask foreigners for advice, claiming that the foreigner knows more than they. Nevertheless they do not really expect the foreigners to agree with the stated shortcomings or to offer advice on issues outside their fields of expertise.

The best response is not to offer any advice except within one's official area of expertise. An American engineer working to develop China's northern oil fields may be asked to comment on China's housing, or to suggest how Chinese factories might be made more efficient. This is the time to be diplomatic and admit ignorance. This is also the time to volunteer that China has many experts of its own, and that a foreigner has little to say that would be useful. After all, the American is not likely to reciprocate and ask how America can reduce its crime rate to that of China's.

Another great temptation for Westerners who have been in China for a short while is to become instant experts on China customs and practices. With a little bit of knowledge, it is tempting to make generalizations that can be blatantly incorrect. Westerners should avoid making pronouncements to Chinese about China. In this case, a little knowledge is very dangerous.

Gift Giving

The exchange of gifts is extremely common in Asian cultures. Gifts are given to celebrate an occasion, as souvenirs of an event, as returns for favors done, or as an investment for future favors. The Chinese are no exception, and almost all social situations demand some gift exchange. Indications of friendship and good character are measured in large part by the gifts given and received.

Gifts in the form of cash should be avoided. Offering money, at best, is seen as unsophisticated and unfeeling; at worst, a money gift can be misunderstood as the offer of a bribe. It also can be seen as an arrogant gesture by a person from a wealthy country to someone in a poorer country. Gifts should be accompanied with a statement of thanks, explaining that the gifts are offered as tokens of thanks to friends who have been helpful.

Foreigners should be hesitant to accept gifts from near-strangers when no event calls for a gift. Gifts given in private—when no third person is present—are also suspect. Such gifts may be personal bribes or payoffs for hoped-for future favors, since the acceptance of a gift entails a future favor in return. It is proper in such instances to refuse a gift by saying that "company policy does not allow me to accept gifts." It is also possible to deflect being the recipient of a potential bribe by accepting the offered object on behalf of the company or other group. This ploy allows the acceptance of a gift without being personally responsible for returning the favor. Later, the donor can be given a return gift in the name of the group that "accepted" the original gift.

Purely business occasions demand gifts from one organization to another. In these instances, one expensive gift is preferable to many gifts given to individuals. These gifts will be displayed with pride in a display case for all to see, including other visitors. A gift to an organization avoids the issue of potential bribes and tipping, both of which are denounced in China. Personal gifts that are received during formal occasions are often given to the organization to be distributed equally or given to more needy members of the group. The last practice, however, is in decline.

To make it easier for members of a delegation to personally receive gifts, a common practice is to place gifts at the place settings for all guests at a banquet. An institutional gift is formally presented, but the personal gifts can be "ignored," especially if they are not expensive and all guests receive the same objects.

Persons who offer inappropriate or inadequate gifts, or who offer no gifts at all, are seen as selfish individuals who do not know how to behave properly. The term *tie-gong-ji,* used to describe a stingy person, literally means "iron rooster"—it is as impossible to get something from a miserly person as it is to get a feather from an iron rooster.

A gift demands a return gift of equal value. It is important to keep lists of gifts received in order to be able to reciprocate. A common practice is to give a second gift a few days after giving the first. The first gift "returns" an earlier gift. The second places a debt on the receiver.

Gifts to individuals should be practical in nature. The Chinese often ask each other what type of gift they would like to receive. Then it is up to the donor to suggest an object similar to one previously received. Foreigners can listen carefully for hints of another's preferences if they feel uncomfortable asking directly.

Foreigners will generally receive gifts that reflect their interests or lifestyles. Chinese hosts are helped greatly when foreign guests suggest which Chinese items they admire. These preferences should be inexpensive, since some gifts will be paid for by the donors themselves rather than by an organization.

Interest in brush ink paintings and scroll works in general shows respect for Chinese culture. The Chinese are flattered when a guest indicates an interest and some knowledge, however slight, of Chinese traditional arts. A Westerner once remarked how good the various teas were in China. By the end of his stay, he had received a number of packets of very good teas. Whenever possible, offer gifts that are personal to the receivers.

Books describing the donor's home country or those written by famous Western contemporary authors are always welcomed by Chinese students and adults in general. If a child of a Chinese host is attending a university, texts in that student's areas of studies are extremely appreciated.

Unlike the Japanese, the Chinese do not value how a gift is wrapped. They believe that a wrapping that is too fancy or better than the object inside makes the donor look cheap. Thus, elegant wrapping go only with elegant gifts.

Gifts such as cans of food (especially fruits), alcoholic beverages, candies, and cakes are always appropriate. One strategy is to give gifts to children, such as toys, games, articles of foreign clothes, and small sums of money wrapped in red paper. Giving to children is equivalent to giving to the parents.

Gifts are seldom given to spouses of business associates. The Chinese separate work from home, and spouses are seldom included in work-related affairs. A gift to a business colleague's spouse is inappropriate unless the spouse is an acquaintance. A gift presented to a spouse when visiting a home is appropriate, but the gift should be for everyone's enjoyment, rather than personal in nature.

The Chinese consider the number *one* to be unlucky. One gift object sometimes defines the donor as stingy. Chinese philosophy stresses harmony and balance, and a sense of completeness is achieved by two rather than one ("things in pairs are like a married couple"). It is appropriate to offer two objects as one gift: two boxes of cookies, or two bottles of liquor. This "rule of two gifts" is not absolute and depends on the value of the gifts being offered. Bringing more than one object is generally the custom, however, though some gifts such as books can stand alone.

Foreigners are allowed to shop at Friendship Stores, government-owned stores that are stocked with tourist items, foreign products, and imported foods unavailable in China. Chinese citizens are generally not allowed to shop in these stores. All purchases must be made with foreign currency or their equivalent. The most appreciated gifts are those found in Friendship Stores, since most of these items are unavailable to ordinary Chinese citizens and have foreign prestige. Friendship Stores are also legitimate sources of appreciated foreign gifts, such as American cigarettes, scotch whiskey, fountain pens, and high quality U.S. maps.

Other welcomed gifts of foreign products include calculators, pens, flashlights (with batteries), alcoholic beverages of any type, fruit, watches, art works, books, and objects that reflect the donor's origin such as national or state flags, or university T-shirts. Flowers are generally unappreciated because they are impractical.

The most treasured gifts are a paid voyage to a foreign country or sponsorship of a child to attend a foreign school. A more common gift is hosting a banquet. Professional reference books are also in great demand in China, since most foreign publications are either unavailable or outdated.

It is best not to open a gift in public. Doing so indicates greed and may embarrass the donor if other gifts are better. At times, however, the donor will insist on opening the package or encouraging the guest to unwrap it. It is then proper to open the gift.

When receiving a gift, it is customary to declare your unworthiness for such a grand gift. When seeing the gift, one should proclaim that the gift is too good but should not show surprise or great excitement. Expressing surprise shows lack of sophistication.

A number of special occasions demand special gifts. During the month-long Spring Festival (Chinese New Year), people visit each other and exchange gifts. Children receive money wrapped in red paper during this festival. Food is the most common type of gift for adults, since each visit involves eating large quantities of food. Stores offer special New Year foods at this time, though any luxury food items are welcomed. If not opened at once, they will be served to the next set of guests or be given to others in turn.

Wedding Gifts

Practical objects are commonly given when a couple marries. Usually, a potential donor checks to see which gifts have already been received. Wedding gifts are presented as early as possible, even weeks before the wedding. Money wrapped in red paper is also given to the bride during the reception. One useful guide for Americans recommends foreign kitchenware or housewares as wedding gifts, since these can be bought in the Friendship Stores and make prestigious gifts.

Other Gifts

Mourning gifts, which include money, are reemerging after being banned during the Cultural Revolution. Cloth— often silk—is a traditional gift at this time.

Visiting the sick in a hospital is almost mandatory. Foreign businesspersons should visit their sick colleagues and close subordinates whenever they stay in a hospital for any length of time. Always take a small gift when visiting the sick. Food, especially fruit, are common gifts.

Gifts commemorating arrivals and departures of any type are customary. Someone leaving for a holiday receives inexpensive gifts from close friends and relatives. Upon returning, this person will offer gifts to complete the exchange.

It is appropriate to offer gifts when a person has experienced a major event, such as acceptance at a prestigious university, graduation, or winning a prize or award. A small gift celebrates the event and indicates your interest in the other's happiness.

Symbolic awards were common in traditional China and are still used extensively today. Communism has been especially adept in honoring persons through symbolic awards, such as a "worker of the month" pin, medal, or banner, or by publishing a worker's name and picture in the local or company newspaper. Factories usually maintain posters exhibiting pictures of exemplary workers.

While, like everyone else, Chinese workers welcome monetary rewards, they also appreciate other forms of rewards. Foreigners managing Chinese should look for ways to show their approval and appreciation for good work. Symbolic awards might include jackets and caps with the company's logo or American-made goods such as picture books, small baskets of food, or alcoholic beverages.

A foreign joint-venture partner should supply its representatives in China with large quantities of items embellished with the company logo or name, such as pens, paper weights, or notepads. Plaques and certificates are also appreciated.

Tipping as a Form of Giving

Tipping is officially forbidden in China, though the custom is reemerging among those who deal with foreigners, such as tourist guides and taxi drivers. Tipping is still considered an insult by many Chinese and is seen as a colonial reminder of foreign exploitation of Chinese labor. Communist ideology stresses that workers provide good service for the honor of the nation rather than for selfish (individual) rewards.

While tipping remains ambiguous, foreigners may nevertheless wish to express their gratitude for special considerations and may have no appropriate gifts available. Some forms of tipping are allowed under limited circumstances.

If one tips, the first rule is never to force money on a reluctant person. There will usually be one or two refusals for the sake of formality and politeness. Further refusals should be accepted, since some Chinese remain hostile toward the practice of cash "gifts."

Second, tipping should be done privately. Tipping is usually an individual reward, which violates the practice of the collective or group reward. The receiver is more likely to benefit from the gift when there are no witnesses. If others are present, the gift may have to be shared equally with other members of the work team. While it is not exactly against the law for a foreigner to offer a tip, it is against the law for a Chinese citizen to accept gratuities. Having witnesses endangers the receiver.

The offering of small gifts (pens, small English-Chinese dictionaries, postcards, caps, or similar items) is often more appropriate than gifts of cash. Very welcome gifts are foreign alcoholic beverages and packages or cartons of American cigarettes. At this time, Marlboro cigarettes are favored in China.

Refusing Gifts

Sometimes it is necessary to reject a gift. A person who is a near stranger or has no reason to be exchanging gifts with you should be told that you are not allowed to receive gifts. Explain as completely as possible that such gifts are against company policy. If you accept a gift, be prepared to perform some favor in exchange. As mentioned before, Chinese etiquette demands a reciprocal exchange of gifts or favors. Each gift implies an obligation of some type.

Inappropriate Gifts

Never give clocks or shoes as gifts. In Chinese, the words *clock* and *death,* and *shoe* and *evil,* have the same pronunciations. As a result, clocks and shoes are seen as gifts that can bring bad luck.

The Chinese are extremely strict in terms of sexual behavior— Communist values are puritanical in extreme. No gifts should contain pornographic material of any type, even if it seem harmless or humorous from a Western perspective. Any art, on calendars or elsewhere (cards, pens, etc.) that shows women in suggestive poses or clothes should not be brought into China, much less offered as gifts. In most cases, this prohibition does not include reproductions of classical Western art showing female figures, though it is difficult to clearly define the line separating "art" from pornography.

Any object with political connotations should also not be brought into China or offered as a gift. Older Chinese remain sensitive about the existence of Taiwan. Gifts made in Taiwan should be avoided in favor of those made in America or in Europe.

Cross-cultural Humor

The Chinese are gracious hosts, and their culture encourages friendly relationships. When encountering this friendliness, Americans often adopt an informal stance. American culture almost demands that, during informal gatherings, the participants exchange jokes and humorous anecdotes. Jokes are signs of informality, equality, and sociability. But Americans often forget that their Chinese hosts may not be proficient enough in English to understand Western humor. Most jokes do not translate well or easily from one language to another. A major nightmare of interpreters is having to instantaneously translate jokes.

In addition, what is funny in one culture may be a serious matter, obscene, or insulting in another. The Chinese, for example, do not appreciate sexual innuendos or jokes of a sexual nature when told in public. The Chinese languages lend themselves to word plays, puns, historical references, and double meanings; however, Western and Asian forms of humor seldom overlap. Novices inexperienced in Chinese culture court social disaster when they attempt humor.

The best position vis-à-vis cross-cultural humor is to indulge in it as little as possible. There is too great a likelihood that a joke will fall flat, be misunderstood, or both. Many jokes are plays on words or use obscure vocabularies, and the humor becomes lost in the Chinese-English language gap.

We recommend being humorous as little as possible at first. More experienced China hands know what humor is appropriate; others should avoid telling jokes at all costs. In any case, the Western practice of beginning a speech with humor is not a Chinese custom, and can easily be omitted.

Smoking

Many Chinese are chain smokers and addicted to cigarette smoking. Meetings rooms are soon filled with tobacco smoke, and a nonsmoker is often in the minority. In fact, many Chinese men will light a second cigarette before the first is completely finished. The first is placed in an ashtray to smolder while the second is being smoked. Often, a person's ashtray will contain three or four smoldering cigarettes, while the individual smokes a fifth. It is considered impolite to ask someone not to smoke, even if the location is one's own office. Nonsmoking zones are nonexistent in China.

Banquets

One of the most frequent gifts in China is food. An invitation to a banquet is a common gift and is enjoyed by all participants. The costs for banquets are met by sponsoring agencies, so the participants enjoy good food at no personal cost. Because housing in China is crowded, foreigners are seldom invited to homes for meals. Few homes can accommodate more than a few guests, and most private kitchens are too small to allow preparation of the numerous dishes demanded by an invitation to dine.

Inviting guests to one's home is taken seriously. In order to be hospitable, the host must offer guests large quantities of food and drinks. Guests are always offered more food than they can consume. There will be as many as ten different dishes.

Chinese food takes extensive preparation, and each dish must be cooked separately and served immediately. A fine meal demands two or more hours of preparation plus more hours of shopping for the freshest materials. It means that one family member must take time from work to shop and cook. During the meal, the host will often be the cook and will not appear until all dishes have been served. Serving food to guests in one's home is demanding and complex.

It is much easier for all concerned to host a banquet in a restaurant or banquet hall, making eating out a central part of gift exchanges. Often, when hosting foreigners, the Chinese will also invite their own friends. This fulfills multiple obligations at one time.

Banquet Seating

The seating order at the banquet table is a very serious protocol issue. For very formal banquets, name cards show the seating arrangement. For less formal banquets, seating is directed by the hosts, though seating arrangements continue to follow a strict protocol. Guests do not sit at the table before being shown their chairs, since choosing one's seat is highly irregular and insulting to the host.

Guests are seated according to rank. Often, seating arrangements become are final only after all guests have arrived, and the host can establish their rank order. For this reason, it is important to arrive exactly on time.

Those unable to attend a banquet at the last minute should warn the host. A messenger may have to be sent to the banquet's location if a telephone call is impossible to complete.

Guests who are members of a group or delegation should arrive together. Such a practice allows the host to welcome all guests in the proper order and make introductions at one time. Tardy guests disturb the welcoming ceremonies. Latecomers also disturb the seating arrangements, since a missing guest forces last-minute seating. It may be difficult to seat a guest who arrives after all others have already been seated. In addition, because restaurants in China close early, hosts dare not delay the beginning of a banquet, and absentees place them in a dilemma. The hosts do not want to delay the banquet, but they also do not want to start if some guests have not arrived. This awkwardness should be avoided at all costs.

Those attending a banquet are distributed equally at tables seating from eight to twelve persons. The Chinese prefer distributing attendees so that tables have equal numbers of diners. Those invited who do not inform the host that they will be absent also threaten this balance.

The guest with the highest rank sits in the seat farthest from and facing the room's door. The host sits at the left of the main guest. If space allows, the main guest's spouse, if present, is seated at the host's left. Other high-ranking guests sit at the host's table if space allows. Interpreters are strategically seated to facilitate conversation. Second-ranked diners (hosts and guests) are seated at another table, using the same general order. The second-ranked host sits on the left of the second-ranked guests, and so forth. If the party is small, generally twelve or less, one table will be used to seat all participants.

Banquet Food

The Chinese begin banquets with cold foods and end with hot soup and rice. The way food is presented is an important element in banquet eating. Room-temperature appetizers are served first, usually arranged in an artistic manner. A common practice is to present the first dishes in the forms of flowers or animals. The shape and color of food arrangements are as important as how the foods taste. One prestigious dish is a river fish that has been cooked and cut into bite-sized pieces then reassembled to form a whole fish. The guests use their serving chopsticks to pick out pieces of fish.

If a banquet takes place in Beijing, a popular banquet fare is Peking duck, the pride of the region's cuisine. There are a number of restaurants that serve only Peking duck and related dishes. A banquet featuring Peking duck begins with cold duck appetizers such as liver and tongue. The next dishes feature other parts of the duck. The main course is the flesh with skin attached. This is eaten with thin pancakes and plum sauce. The last course is duck soup.

Cold dishes are followed by the main meat courses, then the vegetable and seafood platters. The last main course is usually a fish dish, then hot soup and rice. Dessert is often fruit or sweets, but can be omitted.

There will always be six to eight courses in a banquet. For wealthier hosts (or their work units) and more formal occasions, a banquet will include up to fifteen courses. It is important to taste each dish and comment on its beauty and taste.

The main courses are served in large dishes. Each guest will serve or be served from the main dishes. Banquet tables have turntables. The turntable is rotated so that each guest can be served in turn. The task of the serving staff is limited to placing food on the turntables and taking emptied dishes away. Except for state dinners, no one is served by staff.

Each dish is placed in front of the host. He or she takes some food, and then the dish is rotated to the diners. The host generally places food on the main guest's dish and then serves himself. The co-host usually serves the second ranking guest, and so on down the hierarchy.

Guests may also offer to serve a host or co-host by using special serving chopsticks or spoons. Some skill in handling chopsticks is necessary at this stage; however, a foreign guest can request a fork and spoon from the host before the meal begins. The Chinese being served will try to stop the gesture for politeness sake, but the effort is a mark of courtesy. Serving someone's plate is a gift-within-a-gift, since one receives food as a gesture of courtesy.

Chinese food is cut into bite-size pieces in the kitchen, so table settings do not include knives. There will be sets of chopsticks and spoons at each setting. One spoon and a set of chopsticks are set aside to serve food to one's plate and are not used for eating.

The host and colleagues are responsible for serving the guests. Emptied plates are quickly filled up again and again. When a dish is almost gone, the remainder will be offered to a guest. Leaving some food in a plate indicates the diner has had enough. The host will then stop offering or serving food to the guest's plate. If a guest seems to especially like a certain dish, the chances are that some of the contents will be set aside for the guest. There is no Dutch treat in China, and the host is expected to pay for all foods consumed. Not paying the whole tab is seen as extremely impolite. By the same token, people take turns being hosts. The meal you host will be repaid by a meal in exchange at another time. The guest is expected to repay the favor by hosting a meal in exchange or by substituting another favor, such as a gift of some sort. It is best to exchange banquet for banquet, or food for food, though this rule is flexible. For other customs observed in entertaining Chinese, see Exhibit 6-3.

Americans who wish to share the cost of entertaining Chinese guests can settle the bill before or after the event is over. Banquets are usually paid for ahead of time, so the issue of payment is settled before the guests arrive. At the end of a banquet, the host should be saying goodbye to the guests rather than paying the bill. Discussing in public how much should be paid by each host is considered extremely barbaric and will embarrass the guests.

Banquet dishes are ordered a day or two ahead of time, The host orders selected dishes or else determines how many dishes will be served, giving the restaurant managers the freedom to decide on individual dishes. Experienced hosts mention the amount of money they wish to spend on the banquet, and let the restaurant managers determine the number and types of dishes. The bill is paid at the same time these decisions are made.

Banquet Drinking

Drinking any type of alcoholic beverage before a banquet is seldom done. For very formal banquets, the guests are led to a waiting room. Tea and small towels will be offered at this time. Damp towels (hot in winter and cold in summer) are used to wipe the hands. After a few minutes, the guests are led to where the banquet proper will take place.

No drinking takes place until the host has offered a toast. These are usually short and take the form of vague welcoming statements. Beginning toasts sometimes include subtle messages with important implied meanings, such as a hint that an agreement will or will not be soon achieved. Usually, however, they consist of a welcome and a statement of friendship.

Exhibit 6-3. Notes on Entertaining in China

- Never ask if someone has enjoyed a meal. A Chinese guest has to respond positively.

- Offer a cigarette by taking one out of its box and handing it to someone. This keeps the guest from politely declining the offer. The guest may set the cigarette aside or take it home at the end of the evening.

- The host sometimes pays the guests' transportation. Reserve a taxi to take a guest home after a meal. You can also provide transportation to the restaurant. Be at the restaurant to greet your guests.

- Follow a departing guest to a vehicle or the curb of the restaurant. Never say good–bye and shut the door on a guest. Show respect by "walking a guest to the gate."

- Serve a beverage as soon as a guest arrives. Do not ask, but provide the guest with a nonalcoholic drink. Alcoholic drinks are not served as a welcome. Serve tea and soft drinks.

Safe toasts are those announcing friendships of countries, companies, and those present. They can also be pledges of unity and hopes of negotiation success. If the party is large, the host may at times offer toasts at the other tables.

The person or persons being toasted rise to acknowledge the host's toast. The common response to a toast is to say *ganbei* and drink a full glass or cup, which are thankfully smaller in size than those used in the West. The *ganbei* response is a dangerous one, however, since a banquet lasts for a long time and many toasts will be announced and exchanged. It is easy to consume larger-than-expected amounts of alcohol during a banquet of ten or more courses. An alternative response to a toast is *sui-yi* or *sui-bian* ("Please feel free"), which allows a drinker to sip from a glass without draining it.

Some Chinese believe that Westerners are great drinkers and will try, as courteous hosts, to press guests to drink beyond their limits. A guest can always ask for a soft drink, fruit juice, or mineral water in place of alcoholic beverages.

Toasting is common during formal meals, because in China, as in most parts of Asia, a person does not customarily drink alone. Drinking is a social custom, and all present should drink at the same time. Toasting is the way everyone can join in drinking together.

Toasts can be made in honor of the whole table, all present, or to one person. Get the attention of the person you wish to honor and lift your glass, with or without saying anything. Saying something is more polite and personal. Toasting allows both of you to drink, since a toast demands that all participants drink. At intervals, a toast should be offered to everyone present.

Entertaining in the West

Those who entertain Chinese visiting the West should not overwhelm guests with too much foreign food. Many Chinese are unaccustomed to large servings of meat, such as grilled steaks. Some will not feel at ease using Western eating utensils. In addition, the Chinese are among the world's most resistant persons to enjoying foreign foods. Hosting visiting Chinese at a Chinese restaurant in the United States is acceptable and welcomed. Chinese restaurants in most countries have Chinese-language menus offering special dishes. Western hosts can ask for a Chinese-language menu for the guests.

The host orders for all under most circumstances. The custom is to order one dish for each diner, plus a large bowl of soup for everyone. The dishes are passed around so that each person can take a portion from each platter. Ordering one or two extra dishes provides ample amounts of food. A meal should have at a minimum soup, beef, chicken, fish, and shellfish dishes, if there are at least four diners. At least one dish in the Hunan or Sichuan style offers a spicy contrast to the other dishes.

For Further Reading

Devine, Elizabeth, and Nancy L. Braganti. "China," in *The Traveller's Guide to Asian Customs and Manners.* New York: St. Martin's, 1986. 13-42.

McCabe, Robert K. *Guide to Business Travel in Asia.* Lincolnwood, Ilinois: Passport Books, 1987.

Gannon, Martin J., and Associates. *Understanding Global Cultures: Metaphorical Journeys Through 17 Countries.* Thousand Oaks, California: SAFE Publications, 1994.

Hu, Wenzhong, and Cornelius L. Grove. *Encountering the Chinese: A Guide for Americans.* Yarmouth, Maine: Intercultural Press, 1991.

Quanyu, Huang, Richard S. Andrulis, and Chen Tong. *A Guide to Successful Business Relations with the Chinese: Opening the Great Wall's Gate.* New York: International Business Press, 1994.

Selligman, Scott D. *Dealing with the Chinese: A Practical Guide to Business Etiquette in the People's Republic Today.* New York, Warner Books, 1989.

Star, Nancy. *The International Guide to Tipping.* New York: Berkeley Publishing Group, 1988.

7

Living and Working in China

The personality traits of those sent to live and work in China are crucial. Supporting an employee abroad is costly, and the wrong representative can ruin a company's future in China. Also, employees who do not complete their foreign assignment and return to the states early not only disrupt needed relationships with Chinese colleagues but also their own careers.

When making foreign assignments, most American managers first consider the employee's job qualifications. If the individual has the right technical expertise, then all other considerations are secondary; however, surveys indicate that this view is shortsighted and leads to problems. In fact, the emphasis on technical, job-related aptitudes as criteria for foreign assignments is one reason American multinational corporations have the highest rate of expatriate failure in the world.[1] The consideration of job-related talents to the exclusion of other factors courts international failure.[2]

While job-related skills cannot be ignored, they are secondary in importance, when staffing overseas operations. In the first place, work is conducted very differently in various cultures. A successful salesperson in America, for example, would probably be a failure in Japan or China. American sales personnel tend to be individualistic, aggressive, and expressive with their feelings. These characteristics are rejected in Asia, in general, and in China, specifically.

Furthermore, working in a foreign culture is always associated with some degree of *culture shock*—personal stress brought about by being in a foreign social and cultural environment. A person who cannot adjust to new cultural surroundings will most likely be a working failure, regardless of that person's job-related skills and technical expertise.

A possible reaction to culture shock is an unwillingness to associate with host nationals and the cultivation of social ties only with guest nationals (other expatriates). (For a list of personnel terms used in this chapter, see Exhibit 7-1.) Such a person learns little about the host nationals and their culture and works in a cultural vacuum. This leads to intercultural misunderstandings and errors.

Accepting Long-term Assignments

The first consideration in sending an employee overseas is whether a potential expatriate is willing to accept a long-term assignment in China. Those who are willing to go China will have more positive attitudes concerning their assignment. This optimistic outlook reduces the chance of culture shock.

At the very least, willing expatriates see their assignments as adventures and will experience the first two months as a "honeymoon" period. Those who unwillingly find themselves in foreign cultures have no such emotional cushions.

Expatriates need an adjustment period when starting their assignments. Longer periods are needed when the host cultures are particularly alien or unlike the home culture. The expatriate not only has to learn to work with new colleagues whose work styles are different, but being in a new culture demands new solutions to daily living.

Exhibit 7-1. Personnel Terms

Expatriate	A person who lives and works in a foreign nation
Host national	A citizen of a nation
Guest national	A person in a foreign nation
Sojourner	A person in a foreign nation who does not associate with involvement with local culture

---

For example, Chinese food is very unlike Western food, and new arrivals almost always lose weight. Some persons may not be able to adjust to new foods and different ways of buying foodstuffs in the local markets. Many expatriates miss selected dishes not found in the host country. For example, at Beijing University the American students debate constantly about the relative tastes of Chinese and American peanut butter. American students miss pizza, ice cream, fried chicken, and hamburgers the most.

Expatriates face other problems, such as learning how to shop, where needed consumer products can be found, or even whether they are available. A major source of expatriate tension is the reduced living areas available to foreigners. Most foreigners in China find their housing space much smaller than what they are accustomed to at home. Foreigners living in Beijing are restricted to four areas of the city. These are large hotels or series of apartment blocks surrounded by walls. Dining halls are available in the residences, as well as shops stocked with limited foreign commodities. Apartments are small. A one-room apartment has a floor space of roughly 75 square yards. A three-bedroom apartment of 185 square yards costs over US$7,000 a month in Beijing. It is not generally possible for guest nationals to live outside these hotels and compounds, which are set aside specifically for foreigners.

Allowing Time to Adjust

In a survey of ninety-four multinationals, Ingemar Torbiorn found that Swedish employees sent to Asia needed a period of adjustment lasting roughly seven months before reaching full working efficiency. For upper-level managers, the adjustment period generally lasted nine months.[3] A person who does not want to be in China in the first place will not be able to use this adjustment period adequately.

In addition to an employee's willingness to accept a foreign assignment, the employee's family should also be willing to travel. To be effective, assignments to China should last several years. Most newcomers need a period of adjustment to learn how business is conducted in China, to develop personal contacts, and to understand workers and colleagues.

Although overseas employees do not wish to be separated from their families for such a long time, family members often experience great stress as they adjust to living in China. Again, social surveys indicate that a major component of expatriate low morale during a foreign assignment is the degree of unhappiness among family members, especially the spouse's. Pre-teen children generally adapt very well to foreign cultures. In a few months, such children will have already developed a working knowledge of the language and have made new friends. In contrast to adults, children seldom develop adjustment problems.[4]

Spouses have a harder time adjusting to foreign environments than do their working partners because they do not have a familiar focus for their activities. They must adapt to new modes of living, often in unpleasant conditions, and they cannot escape by working for eight or more hours a day. Thus, nonworking spouses face the twin problems of boredom and coping with a foreign environment.

Expatriates in China usually work longer hours than they do at home, in part because there is so little else for foreigners to do. The high cost of supporting an expatriate staff in China usually results in understaffing, resulting in more responsibilities for those who are there.

Limited Opportunities for Leisure Activities

It is difficult, though not impossible, to integrate with Chinese society to any meaningful extent without some local language facility. Nonworking spouses may have the opportunity to teach a foreign language—especially English—on a volunteer basis, but there is usually little opportunity for other activities. Chinese laws do not allow spouses to work for pay during their stay in China. This regulation is being relaxed, but those who enter China without work find it difficult to obtain work permits. As one former expatriate advises, "Bring lots of board games."

Studies and hobbies are possible activities, though most Western hobby enthusiasts have difficulty finding adequate supplies in China. Many organized activities for foreigners are available in Shanghai and Beijing. Embassies also form clubs and associations for their expatriates. These are good sources of support for newcomers.

In most of China's cities, foreigners can find tutors who are willing to teach Mandarin, Chinese art forms, Tai Chi exercises and various martial arts, and Chinese cooking. In more isolated areas, Chinese students or English language teachers are usually available and willing to teach language courses, but few other activities may exist. In fact, finding resources for leisure activities is a major problem faced by expatriates in China. Though leisure facilities are slowly becoming available, only a handful of golf courses and swimming pools presently exist. Even expatriate joggers find that running in China's polluted cities can be dangerous to their health.

The family living overseas must be emotionally close and supportive. Family members will be forced to rely on each other more than they do in their home country. Families that are dysfunctional in any aspect can break down very quickly in a foreign environment. Alcoholism and divorce can be some of the costs of foreign assignments.

Special Employee Characteristics

Certain characteristics should be looked for when selecting an employee for duty in China or when considering going oneself. One study found that the best person to send is someone who is highly *diplomatic*.[5] Diplomats are flexible within certain limits. They focus on attaining objectives rather than by stressing the means of achieving these goals. They can therefore compromise and adjust their behavior as conditions change.

Diplomats also stress the human elements of a situation. They are alert to cues, including oral and body languages, that suggest whether a certain proposal or course of action is acceptable. Diplomats work well with and through others. Their communication skills are superior, even in multicultural settings.

Another vital personality characteristic is the *willingness to learn*. When dealing with fellow nationals, individuals can assume that all parties generally understand each other, and that everyone has about the same cultural resources. Nothing should be assumed when dealing with foreigners, including the Chinese. The person who can best deal with such cultural and social ambiguities is someone willing to learn everything and assume nothing.

Another useful personal characteristic for expatriate managers is *willingness to teach*. Chinese workers and managers are eager to learn Western methods of business in order to develop world-class abilities. Foreigners who are willing to assume the role of teachers as they deal with their subordinates will gain the good will and the gratitude of Chinese.

On-the-job teaching demands *patience*. It also demands that all operations include training, even though such a policy reduces productivity in the short run. An expatriate who practices patience, rather than assuming that all directives will be instantly understood and obeyed, is more likely to be successful. This person will be given great face by the Chinese, which will facilitate a wide range of endeavors.

As mentioned previously, the cost of maintaining expatriates in China is so great that the staff in China will almost always be short-handed. As a consequence, expatriates should teach host nationals some corporate procedures in order to standardize reporting, accounting, and other administrative activities and to reduce their own heavy work loads.

Expatriates also find they have to assume new responsibilities and make more decisions. Working in a foreign country enlarges the scope of any job. Those who do not want greater responsibilities should not accept foreign assignments.

Self-confidence

Persons who are confident that they can solve problems as they arise will also be more likely to succeed in a foreign assignment. Self-confident individuals are more likely to observe, learn, and copy. They are more willing to learn from cultural mentors and cultural mediators. To those individuals, unfamiliarity is a challenge and an opportunity rather than a threat to their egos. They have the self-confidence to adapt to new cultural demands. At the same time, multinational corporate officials in the home country should be willing to "forgive" expatriates' early errors and allow for some experimentation.

Those who lack self-confidence will be too afraid of failure to try to learn new behavior. They are more likely to withdraw into the expatriate community—become sojourners—and to interact as little as possible with host country nationals.

All expatriates make mistakes. Even experienced China hands make errors in language and behavior. Self-confident persons are less likely to let mistakes discourage them because they understand that these experiences are part of learning by trial and error.

Tolerating Social and Cultural Ambiguity

The best persons—employees and family members—to send abroad are those who tolerate and adjust well to social and cultural ambiguity. A person who is rigid and unyielding will not succeed in China. As noted elsewhere, the Chinese sense of time differs from that of the West. Work goals are achieved in China but often at a pace different from one expected by a foreigner. Nor does a foreigner always know when a "yes" should be interpreted as a "no" or perhaps as a "maybe."

Coping With the Language

If one doesn't mind being lost or confused at times, living in China does not demand a knowledge of the local language, though it is a great advantage. Predeparture preparation should include some language lessons. Knowledge of a few words and phrases are useful to begin conversations and to indicate a respect for the host culture. Shops catering to foreigners have ample supplies of phrase books and dictionaries for sale.

Foreigners who do not read any Chinese characters are at a loss, since many stores do not have display windows, and all signs use ideograms. Unless a guide is available, a foreigner needs to look into each store in order to find the one stocking needed consumer goods.

Hotels and other places catering to foreigners have personnel who speak foreign languages, though their knowledge may be rudimentary. Restaurants in international hotels offer English language menus. Chinese opera theaters provide foreign language translations. However, there are few movies in China that offer English subtitles, and most Chinese know few foreign words.

Chinese clerks generally are patient with foreigners who stumble for the correct words, though they may laugh a little and call their friends to watch this spectacle. In such cases, a good pocket dictionary is useful to point out key words and phrases.

Immigrant Chinese Employees

Ideal employees to send to China are immigrant Chinese or their descendants, especially if the latter are familiar with Chinese culture. Most Chinese Americans are descendants of Chinese living on the coast or in the Guangzhou area (Canton) in the province of Guangdong and may speak Cantonese rather than Mandarin. A firm with Chinese-American employees has a great advantage over those who do not. Many Chinese Americans will have family ties in China.

An estimated 800,000 overseas Chinese live in the United States, and 289,000 in Canada. A number of these Chinese are students who will eventually wish to return to their homeland, though even these will want to stay in the United States and Canada if they can find employment.[6] Other potential pools of Chinese- and English-speaking overseas Chinese are found in Australia (122,000); New Zealand (19,000); and the United Kingdom (91,000). Not all of these overseas Chinese may want to return to work in China, nor will many be familiar with local languages and customs. However, the potential of these Chinese in English-speaking countries should not be overlooked.

Preparing for the Assignment

A successful foreign assignment demands careful preparation. A carefully constructed predeparture program can also uncover personality traits that preclude someone from going on a foreign assignment. The most beneficial predeparture programs include prospective expatriates and their family members.

Predeparture programs include *cultural, utilitarian,* and *work-oriented* elements. *Cultural* elements provide a general introduction to the host culture, including literature on the society and its arts, history, and national character. Information on the host national culture is essential, and allows trainees to learn about the value systems and personality profiles of the host society. Included in this information are discussions of taboos and general etiquette. Certain gestures, for example, are defined as obscene by Chinese but not by Westerners.

Another aspect of Chinese culture is food. Adjustment to a new culture is made somewhat easier when an expatriate is at least somewhat familiar with local foods. Prospective expatriates need to be familiar with some of the local dishes and their ingredients. A few lessons on how and what to eat ease the transition for newcomers. Often, a completely different diet and new eating patterns are disorienting. In addition, new expatriates find that many foodstuffs are unfamiliar. Local mentors can guide newcomers through the local markets and teach them how to use unfamiliar fruits, vegetables, and other food products.

Familiar food is an important source of emotional stability, and expatriates who live in China's larger cities periodically go to international hotels to enjoy Western-style meals. If an expatriate family expects to have cooking facilities while in China, a few favorite prepackaged dishes should be taken along. These might include cartons of pizza ingredients, favorite sauces and mixes, or even freeze-dried meals.

Utilitarian information deals with the daily problems faced by long-term residents. Most guide books offer information for short-term visitors, such as tourists, and cover such issues as tipping and acceptable clothing. Long-term residents, however, must learn how to cope with landlords, shopping, and local transportation systems. Other necessary information includes how to locate consumer products that are difficult to find in China. A useful strategy for someone who is the first to live in an area is to keep a diary for replacements to use as a reference.

American students studying at Beijing University establish communication with those coming later in the same program. Newcomers fit in very well, since they bring the latest music and the requested jars of peanut butter, one of the foods American students miss the most.

Lists of unavailable products are needed in the predeparture planning stages of the trip (see Exhibit 7-2). Larger cities in China can meet most of a foreigner's needs, though smaller urban centers lack much of what Westerners consider necessary for daily living.

Petroleum company employees working in northern China will find few Western articles on the local market or even in stores catering to foreigners. For example, few Chinese smoke pipes. Pipe tobacco is seldom found in China's smaller cities. Foreigners who smoke pipes often must use cigarette tobacco unless they plan ahead. A family may have to bring a three-month supply of disposable diapers or infant food because none are available locally. When their own supplies run out, some expatriates may have to travel to Hong Kong for special products, such as medicine, eyeglasses, books, or computer supplies.

Maps of the prospective residential area with notations for stores that welcome foreigners or offer special goods are useful. Maps

---

Exhibit 7-2. Essentials to Take with You

What to Take

All paper products	Instant coffee
Cigarettes	Pipe tobacco
Batteries	Flashlights
Peanut butter	Paperbacks
Medicines	First aid items
Drinking cups	Warm clothes
Favorite jams	Chewing gum
Birthday and Christmas gifts	

should also pinpoint schools, medical offices, and other essential locations. One very useful map traces certain bus and subway routes, with bus numbers and correct fares indicated. Such information saves newcomers much time and stress. These local maps cannot be purchased but are made on the spot by more experienced China hands and given to newcomers.

Other practical information includes names and addresses of language tutors, drivers, dependable baby-sitters, and English-speaking physicians. Often, a newcomer "inherits"—from a previous expatriate— special treatment and goodwill from shopkeepers. Such advanced information can shorten a newcomer's adjustment period. Of course, newcomers can also inherit bad feelings developed by "ugly" predecessors. In such cases, newcomers must overcome the negative label. This situation can make the first period of a foreign assignment more difficult than necessary.

Work-oriented information is whatever information a newcomer must have in order to function well in a work setting. This information includes names, addresses and descriptions of the power structure at the workplace. Generally, the most influential persons in an organization are members of the local executive council of the Chinese Communist Party (CCP). Who these persons are may not be evident in an official organization diagram. Often, selected supervisors have influence beyond their official jurisdiction. These linchpins need to be identified if the newcomers are to become effective managers. Also important to new or potential expatriates is information on the culture of work in China. Ignorance of how work is actually conducted will almost certainly lead to frustration and inefficiency.

Most newcomers are idealistic when they begin an assignment. They are often naive in terms of how much change they will actually be able to introduce. Westerners, in particular, assume that their work methods are best or that Chinese workers are willing to become completely "Western" in their behavior. The most effective expatriate is someone who adjusts a little to Chinese work customs.

The Adjustment Cycle

The adjustment to living in a new culture involves a cycle with four stages: *honeymoon, disillusionment, adjustment,* and *mastery.*[7] The *honeymoon* stage, lasting up to two months, begins as the expatriate first experiences the host culture. Differences between host and home cultures are seen as exciting and interesting, and the expatriate romanticizes the new culture so all new experiences are positive.

During this stage, the newcomer is essentially a protected tourist—a visitor—who is a spectator rather than a participant or player. Usually, the Chinese carefully guide newcomers so that they experience only positive elements of the local culture. The Chinese hosts control events, so the newcomer feels that the host culture is easily understood and approachable. Thus, newcomers often feel they have become "experts" after a few weeks.

However, with continued experience, the differences between the native and the host cultures begin to irritate rather than to amuse, and some degree of *disillusionment* begins. Culture shock develops at this time. The expatriate is no longer protected and now attempts to cope alone with the host culture. The problems of daily living eventually may wear down even the most enthusiastic newcomer.

With time, new arrivals begin to notice the pollution, the noise, and the constant crowds. The local culture no longer seems so benign and easily handled. Expatriates begin to realize that misunderstandings exist and that the culture is more of a mystery than anticipated. In the workplace they begin to notice differences in work styles between themselves and the Chinese nationals and to realize that these differences will not disappear quickly.

The third stage, *adjustment,* begins as the expatriate gradually adapts to the local culture and learns to appreciate its complexity. This adaptation develops through learning, often by making mistake after mistake. Increasingly, the ordinary decisions of daily living no longer loom as big problems.

Individuals achieving the adjustment stage know where to get haircuts and needed foods. They know where the closest free markets and restaurants are located. The world begins to be familiar again, and though tensions always exist, growing familiarity offers more independence and a sense of control.

The last stage, *mastery,* occurs only after a few years of residency. The problems of working and living in China are solved, or accepted if they cannot be changed. The expatriate accepts the cultural differences and may even recognize the superiority or attractiveness of segments of the host culture. During this stage, expatriates may take lessons in Chinese brush painting or learn to negotiate comfortably with Chinese partners. They may even decide that their experiences improve their careers and that being in China offers many advantages.

Unfortunately, many expatriates return home before reaching the mastery stage. A better policy on the part of companies is to shorten the adjustment cycle through careful and thorough predeparture training and to extend the foreign assignment. In this way, the position is filled for two or more years by an adjusted, effective expatriate.

Imposing Western Values on China

An unfortunate tendency, which almost ensures that expatriates will not adjust, is that of judging the Chinese and China by Western standards. The vast differences between Chinese and American societies almost demand comparison, usually to the disadvantage of the Chinese. This results from the inability of newcomers to separate Chinese values and behavior from those of their home country.

Expatriates often become angry at behavior and conditions that are different from those at home. They evaluate host culture differences as inferior and idealize their native culture. Soon, all differences become personal attacks on Western and personal values and standards. Such an attitude precludes accepting inconveniences and unfamiliarity with patience and humor.

By contrast, one expatriate family lived in an apartment with inadequate heating. In one bedroom, however, the heater could raise the room's temperature to 57 degrees Fahrenheit. This made the other bedroom cold by comparison. The family members did not complain, since their Chinese colleagues had even worse accommodations. The family successfully adjusted, bought more blankets, and slept and lived together in one room until spring came.

Discomforts in China should be seen in the larger context of existing conditions, rather than at the personal level. China remains a third world country in many respects, and foreign residents enjoy a standard of living unavailable to most Chinese. Actually, many of these discomforts are magnified out of proportion because of the unfamiliar cultural environment and are the result of subjective evaluations rather than actual conditions.

Cultural Rehearsals

A technique that shortens the disillusionment stage and reduces the time needed to achieve a sense of mastery is the *cultural rehearsal.* This consists of role-playing by future expatriates and members of the host culture. Leaders in role-playing sessions can also include

Westerners who have firsthand experience in China. The prospective expatriate acts out various activities and the host nationals respond in a typical manner.

One possible scenario is a mock interview with job applicants. The Chinese present themselves as humble and modest and are reluctant to boast about their skills. The trainee learns during a cultural rehearsal how to best elicit information in order to judge a job applicant. The Chinese team members review the trainee's mistakes and suggest changes.

Another useful exercise employs a mock negotiation session. The Chinese members act out Chinese-style negotiating behavior while the trainee responds. Such review sessions prepare the trainee for actual negotiations.

Mock dramas that help future expatriates can also include role-playing for shopping, asking directions, and work activities. Prospective expatriates pretend to deal with Chinese colleagues and subordinates. Rehearsals teach the trainees how to give orders, how to learn bad news, and how to receive advice. Rehearsals also alert trainees to differences in body language, and other behavior. Sessions, sometimes held at Chinese restaurants, may include learning how to eat with chopsticks and proper banquet behavior.

Host country nationals (HCNs) are vital resources in the adjustment process. They can become valuable assets as cultural guides as well as work colleagues. Experienced HCNs who are familiar with the cultures involved can teach expatriates how to adjust in the least-painful manner.

Look-See Visits

A useful strategy to test whether a prospective expatriate will do well in China or elsewhere is a look-see visit to the host country. That is, trainees are sent to live in China for short periods. They have little or no job responsibilities. Instead, the trainees immerse themselves in the local culture and learn the local customs.

Samsung Company, a major Korean multinational corporation, prepares future expatriates by offering language lessons and cultural programs. Trainees then go to China, live with Chinese families to learn local lifestyles, and receive on-the-job training. They then return to the home office for more training to prepare for future, long-term assignments in China.

Many Japanese companies also include similar pre-assignment visits to foreign nations. German corporations send senior executives to isolated parts of China to receive language lessons and to learn how to adapt to living in Chinese society without the support of an expatriate community. An alternative is to expect a prospective expatriate and family to take a vacation in the country of assignment.

American companies could also provide early visits of various lengths for trainees and family members to test their responses to being in a foreign culture. Look-see visits offer a realistic training environment to prepare trainees for longer stays. Unfortunately, most U.S. multinationals do not expend these kinds of resources on future expatriates. Nevertheless, early visits reduce assignment failures and early returns. They also shorten the adjustment cycle needed by expatriates to reach the mastery level.

Look-see visits are also extremely beneficial for expatriates' spouses. As mentioned earlier, the major reason for assignment failure among U.S. expatriates is the unhappiness of family members, especially of the spouse. One expatriate's pregnant wife arrived in Beijing without a look-see visit and soon determined that local medical facilities were inadequate. She decided to return home immediately, leaving her spouse alone and knowing he would miss the birth of his first child. Needless to say, he was not an effective employee. A predeparture visit would have avoided this problem. Wives can also use look-see visits to check educational facilities for children, to evaluate housing, and to find out about other essential items.

In addition, a short visit allows spouses the chance to learn exactly what needs to be packed or sent. These trips also provide information more experienced expatriates forget to tell newcomers. Procter & Gamble sends prospective expatriates and spouses to Beijing for two months for language and cultural training before they are officially sent on a foreign assignment.

In the past, a common practice of U.S. multinationals was to send the working spouse, at that time mostly husbands, abroad three to six months ahead of family members. The assumptions were that new expatriates would not have to worry about family responsibilities and would have work to fill their days, thus avoiding culture shock. They could also prepare for their family members' later arrival, alert them about what to pack, and generally cushion the shock of their first foreign experiences.

This has not been an especially effective policy. When the employees and their families are separated, employees face the challenge of early adjustment by themselves. Also, with the heavy work responsibilities in China, the employee does not have enough time to thoroughly prepare for the family's arrival, so many problems remain unsettled. In addition, an individual living alone does not confront the same problems experienced later on by family members.

Cultural Mentors

Preparation for foreign assignment ideally includes establishing a mentor-trainee relationship between a newcomer and a more experienced colleague. The responsibility of the mentor is to familiarize a new or potential expatriate with the specific problems of living and working abroad. It is best if the mentor is the newcomer's predecessor, though this may not be possible.

If at all possible, foreign assignments should overlap so that a replacement can learn on site from someone who has already coped with the problems the newcomer will face. A colleague who has lived at the work destination is also preferable. The mentor essentially relays personal experience and offers advice.

Whenever possible, all family members should be involved with mentors. If the husband is the working spouse, he can easily receive advice from a colleague. Wives can also benefit from the personal knowledge and experience of another woman who has spent a year or more at the destination.

Working spouses generally focus on the problems at work, since those are their responsibilities and their careers. The needs of spouses are often ignored or seen as secondary. "Support spouses" prepare newcomers for the special problems involved in a foreign assignment.

The mentor-newcomer tie benefits both partners. For the employee about to be transferred, the mentor gains a temporary ally at the home office. Until the newcomer arrives, at least one colleague serves as an official tie with the expatriate. One useful exchange of favors is for the future newcomer to send office gossip and information in exchange for information on the foreign assignment. Mentoring can go in both directions, forming a more even and more mutually beneficial exchange of information.

Host country nationals can also become cultural mediators. Knowing the culture of each person, HCNs can "translate" requests, orders, and expectations from one party or another.

Imagine that a Chinese employee wishes to ask for extra holidays to travel to another part of China to attend a cousin's wedding or funeral. This worker may find it difficult to explain to a Westerner that this cousin is a favorite of the head of his extended family, and that attending the function is an act of filial devotion. The worker may also feel embarrassed to say that travel is difficult in China, and that it may take several days to reach the destination and to return.

A cultural mediator can point out to the expatriate superior that this ceremony is important and that the worker should be given a bonus or salary advance so that he can offer gifts to the appropriate relatives. Many companies maintain welfare funds so that employees can borrow small amounts of money for such special purposes.

Living In China

Expatriates and their family members find that living in China, although exciting, is also difficult and challenging. China is not a consumer- or leisure-oriented society in the Western sense. A major complaint of expatriates is the lack of leisure activities. Until a few years ago, China had no night clubs, except those in international hotels, and there were few leisure activities after dusk. Even today, China remains very puritanical, and those leisure activities that exist are usually family- and home-oriented.

Chinese government officials wish to cater to the needs of foreigners yet keep them isolated from the general society. In addition, as has been discussed, China remains a tightly controlled socialist economy that foreigners cannot easily penetrate. With few private residences in China, for example, foreigners cannot live wherever they wish. Nor would China's leaders want foreigners to freely choose their residences and neighbors.

Housing and Local Transportation

The Friendship Hotels and Friendship Stores are the result of the government's desire to please and to isolate foreigners. Nontourist foreigners generally live in Friendship Hotels. These are large complexes—based on a Soviet model—which concentrate the residences allotted for foreigners into limited areas. These are walled with guarded gates, thereby facilitating control and observation.

In spite of the restricted atmosphere, the Friendship Hotel simplifies housing problems for foreigners. Housing is at a premium in China, and foreigners would have difficulty finding adequate housing and office space on their own. A private housing market in China barely exists, and foreigners are seldom allowed to enter this market except for business purposes. Foreigners are not allowed to own land except under restrictive conditions in the Special Economic Zones.

Friendship Hotels provide, as best as is possible, Western-style living arrangements. The complexes are large, with some shopping and dining facilities. In the past, many foreign representatives had offices in their hotel suites or rooms. Office facilities are more plentiful now, though there are still relatively few office buildings available for foreigners.

It is common for a foreign company to rent one or more hotel suites or rooms for office use. This practice results in an expatriate living and working in the same hotel. Most rooms have little or no cooking areas, so that all meals are eaten in local restaurants or business clubs. This further isolates foreigners from informal, nonwork-related contact with the Chinese.

The Chinese sometimes allow the employees of foreign joint ventures with Chinese factories to live in Friendship Hotel-type residences on the factory grounds. This hotel-like arrangement is frequently uncomfortable for expatriates and their families, who are used to larger, more private living quarters. Few expatriates working in China have single-family residences.

Predeparture preparation should include thorough information on living arrangements. Some expatriates and family members may not be able to endure cramped, hotel living unless prepared to do so. Remember that there is relatively little for expatriates to do in China, and much more time is spent in one's apartment than is usual for most Westerners. Most of China is bitter cold during the winter months, further ensuring that expatriates spend time in their apartments or hotel lobbies. Unacceptable housing increases the chances of work failures, family tensions, and early return.

Friendship Stores were also established to provide foreigners with rationed or scarce goods not generally available to the average Chinese citizen and to make imported goods available to those who could use foreign currencies. Friendship Stores service only foreigners, and all goods and services are paid in foreign currency or its equivalent in foreign exchange certificates, a special currency established by the Chinese government for exchange with foreign currencies. Chinese currency cannot be exchanged for foreign currencies. This dual currency system is due to be phased out when the Chinese yuan becomes fully convertible into foreign currencies, but the date so far remains indefinite.

Friendship Stores offer ordinary, everyday essentials, including household and kitchen items, small appliances, foreign literature, medicines, and clothing, as well as luxury tourist goods. Larger Friendship Stores have grocery stores where foods—local and foreign—are available. Few foreign goods are easily available outside the Friendship Stores.

Local Travel

Western expatriates are members of automobile-using cultures, where owning and using autos are taken for granted. Cars offer few problems in the West and in North America are the most common method of transportation. The opposite is true in China, where automobiles are a new phenomenon, and where there are still very few private autos. In fact, until a few years ago, it was illegal to own a private automobile in China. Cars are not yet generally considered individual property. They belong to a firm or office, and most are driven by chauffeurs. Foreign companies are allowed small fleets, but they are designated as company property and must be driven by officially appointed drivers. The private use of automobiles has only begun in China, generally in the Special Economic Zones.

Nor can private citizens or foreigners take a drive on a whim. There are few public service stations and almost no available mechanics. Until recently, expatriates and embassy personnel employed full-time mechanics to make repairs. Foreign businesspersons often used mechanics from their embassies. In Shenyang, a city of four million, there are fewer than thirty gasoline stations. This lack of mobility further increases the sense of isolation and restriction felt by expatriates and their families. Any travel beyond their immediate neighborhood is a major undertaking.

Local travel is made possible primarily by public transportation. Bus systems are extensive in large cities, although buses become extremely overcrowded during peak periods. The bus systems are fairly easy for a foreigner to understand. During rush hours, the Chinese forget to maintain their usually calm public deportment and will push and crowd into buses. A foreigner usually has to fight for entry like anyone else. The driver or ticket puncher will usually displace a rider to give a foreign guest a seat, unless the bus is so crowded that no movement is possible.

Because most large Chinese cities are built on level terrain, the Chinese use bicycles to travel short distances, and there are often more lanes set aside for cyclists than for automobile drivers. Long-term resident foreigners quickly obtain bicycles, sometimes from expatriates who are ending their own China assignments, and use them for short trips. We recommend that those packing to go to China include a bicycle repair kit and metric tools as needed equipment.

Some Chinese cyclists are as aggressive as automobile drivers found in any Western capital city, and there are enough automobiles in the central road lanes to create problems for bicyclists. While bicycling in Beijing, the senior author often chose to follow an older person. This did not work when the person followed showed no fear or consideration for others and zipped in and out of lanes to pass.

Foreigners generally use taxis when traveling in large Chinese cities. Drivers can be hired for half or full days for more extensive outings. Taxis do not patrol the streets for customers, and most can be found only in front of the large hotels catering to foreigners. It is also possible to telephone for a taxi, though the wait may be long. It is more convenient to hire a taxi for several hours and have the driver wait while you conduct business or shop. The rate for waiting is low.

Semi-official taxis in the form of vans driven by entrepreneurs are a recent addition. The vans follow general routes with detours for passengers. Passengers must negotiate fares and routes with the drivers and, therefore, must know Chinese. Vans are not recommended transportation for novice expatriates.

It is still impossible for individuals to buy round-trip tickets for train and plane travel. As a consequence, much time can be spent waiting in line for return tickets. Although travel agencies do provide such services, they are usually limited to guided tours.

Most foreigners in China are guests of some official bureau or state-owned enterprise. These generally have a Foreign Affairs Office that can arrange for outings, tours, special guides, and other amenities. Foreign Affairs Office personnel can get tickets for cultural and sport events, provide transportation, and generally facilitate the enjoyment of leisure activities. Some offices also provide access to international telephone operators and mailing services. Newcomers should ask about the existence of the Foreign Affairs Office and its activities. Most of these offices publish notices of sponsored activities at locations where foreigners eat or frequently pass by, but a newcomer should ask where notices are posted.

Self-help Groups

Expatriates tend to cluster together in any country. This is more likely in China, where most foreigners are housed in close proximity. Living in China is more pleasant when expatriates form mutual support groups. More experienced members of such networks can give valuable advice to newcomers.

Whenever possible, expatriate supervisors should adopt a policy requiring (1) that all employees join support groups, and (2) that established expatriates be responsible for helping newcomers. In fact, reward systems should be put into place to encourage such partnerships. Self-help groups make expatriate work failure and culture shock less likely. As we pointed out earlier, experienced colleagues are excellent sources of information. Joining a network containing more experienced expatriates makes adjustment much easier.

Members of one recently arrived family were overjoyed when the youngest child was told where the "M&M store" was, and where the best Chinese peanut butter could be found. The child could then obtain his favorite foods, which he greatly missed. That the expiration date on M&M packages was six months overdue was no problem. The child was soon able to go get his candy by himself. The boy also quickly learned to speak a number of words in Mandarin and was able to help his mother shop in the local markets.

Sojourners

The successful expatriate worker must, however, strike a balance between going-it-alone and complete involvement in the expatriate community. A typical reaction to the strangeness of a foreign culture is *avoidance*. Those who experience culture shock retreat from the host culture and spend as much time possible with other expatriates. They interact with the local culture as little as possible. This is more likely for those who do not speak the local language.

Such persons are *sojourners:* people who are "passing through" a foreign culture with a minimum of impact. Cultural and political realities encourage a sojourner stance when Westerners live in China. A retreat into the expatriate community is protective and comfortable, but it does not allow a person to develop an accurate knowledge of the host culture and its members. In addition, small issues can assume great importance in the small, intense expatriate community. Sojourners who become completely involved in the expatriate community may find themselves in a situation that requires taking sides. These intracommunity conflicts can destroy harmony at work and lower morale in general, as everyone takes sides in what in a normal context would be considered petty issues.

By refusing to adapt to some extent to the host culture, sojourners try to isolate themselves as much as possible from contact with host nationals and become increasingly ineffective when dealing with them. Sojourners' negative attitudes and hostility are good predictors of foreign assignment failure and early return. Self-help groups, to be effective, should help expatriates adjust to their new environment, not avoid it.

Almost as harmful to morale are expatriates who "go native." These are foreigners who reject the expatriate community and interact as little as possible with its members. The community loses a valuable source of knowledge, since these persons can be excellent mentors and cultural resource persons. These individuals should be integrated into the expatriate community as much as possible.

Discovering China

Expatriates who don't have mentors can with some effort learn how to cope with the problems of daily living in China. One method is to walk through the local neighborhood and peek in any store whose functions are not easily understood. The adventurous explorer, with some courage, can easily discover which goods and services each store has to offer. There is no need to be shy. Since few stores have window displays, expatriates not able to read the stores' signs can only look in and take note. The Chinese do not mind foreigners entering their shops, and their reactions are likely to be amusement.

China does not have a fully developed consumer society. Yet many stores and market stalls offer nonessential goods. Foreigners in China can achieve a sense of self-reliance and control by learning how to shop in their immediate residential areas. One of the first excursions an expatriate should make is a tour of the surrounding residential area, noting all stores.

On one such trip, the senior author discovered a small covered market that sold excellent tea, chocolate, and fresh fruit. There was also a calligrapher who offered excellent-quality brushwork. After finding a tea he liked, the author asked his part-time interpreter to go with him to the market to determine the name of the tea. The interpreter wrote the name of the tea in Chinese ideograms, and this paper was presented whenever the author wanted to buy that particular tea. This was a source of amusement to the clerks. The note would be passed around to show fellow clerks what the foreigner wanted.

A note about children. The Chinese love children. Infants are spoiled and under constant care until they are old enough to attend school. Foreigners with young children are targets of attention, and children are catered to (or spoiled) by Chinese shopkeepers and passersby. A child is often the entry for special treatment as well as attention.

Sending Women Employees to China

Women can be sent on assignments in China. All adults in China are employed except the handicapped and the retired. Socialist ideology stresses gender equality, and while relatively few Chinese women are found at the higher bureaucratic and managerial levels, they are common in the middle and lower levels. Most women in China work outside the home during most of their lives, and very few are unemployed housewives. Most women contribute to their families' incomes before and after marriage.

One researcher found that women may have advantages in foreign cultures that demand sensitivity to cultural values and interpersonal relations.[8] The Chinese welcome foreigners skilled at cross-cultural communication who are also alert to Chinese customs and behavior. It is much better for an American firm to send a female employee who can adapt to being in China or who is familiar with Chinese culture and society than to assign a male who is not sensitive to Chinese etiquette and customs. The latter has a much greater probability of adjustment failure.

The Chinese define female working expatriates as foreign company representatives, first; as foreigners, second; and as females, last. They treat female expatriates with the same courtesy they offer all foreigners in good standing. An American executive should not hesitate to send a female employee to China who is qualified and wishes to go.

Working in China

China is a hardship zone for most expatriates. They generally work long hours and have little free time. There is little for foreigners to do in China, especially when they have no language facilities.

Going for a walk or a long bicycle ride is tiring because China's cities are extremely polluted, and there is little to do at the end of a journey. Most leisure activities take place in hotels or nearby clubs and embassies. Many recently built residence hotels have tennis courts, movie theaters, and similar facilities. With less than one hundred swimming pools in all of China, hotels and national clubs offer the few swimming and leisure facilities available to foreigners.

Movies attended by the Chinese public are cheap but lack foreign subtitles. Larger cities offer a variety of entertainment, such as Chinese opera, sports events, circuses, variety shows, and puppet shows. Nevertheless the activities and tourist facilities available in Shanghai or Beijing are fewer than those found in Western capitals and metropolitan areas. As mentioned earlier, China is neither a consumer-oriented nor a leisure-oriented society.

Doing business in China is extremely time-consuming, especially during the early stages when an expatriate is inexperienced. Those in a home-country office, who have never experienced an assignment in China, seldom realize how confusing and slow business activities can be. An expatriate must work long hours and spend an inordinate amount of time developing a wide range of personal relationships. Expatriates also work long hours to show progress to their superiors. An activity that takes two or three months to settle in Western Europe or North America may demand two or more years to finalize in China. Those not familiar with business practices in China do not understand such problems. Unfortunately, senior U.S. corporate officals seldom are familiar with Chinese business procedures.

Expatriates also work long hours because of the cost of living in China. China is a third world nation, and basic costs are cheap for the Chinese; however, foreigners pay a premium for everything. The average cost of maintaining a representative in China for a year, aside from salary and bonuses, can be as much as $200,000, primarily because of housing costs, which are usually not negotiable.

Since space is at a premium, most foreigners have little choice other than to live and work in hotels for foreigners. An office converted from a hotel room costs $50,000–$125,000 annually, depending on the hotel. When available, office space costs $25–$50 per square meter per month and has increased in average cost from 1992 to 1995. Joint-venture partners have lower costs, since they maintain offices at local factories or central office buildings. But these are generally located large distances from the center of the business district, so offices in more centrally located hotels are usually necessary.

The high costs of supporting a staff in China also add an urgency for expatriates to show progress and to complete current projects. This, in turn, increases the motivation of expatriates to work longer hours. Long workweeks, unfortunately, threaten family relations, thereby causing another set of problems.

The Positive Side

Commercial success in China is possible, and many expatriates enjoy their stay in China and relish the various challenges they face, usually successfully. Good working relationships with Chinese colleagues are possible, and the basic Chinese national character is friendly and gregarious. Historically, a large number of foreigners have become totally captivated by China's culture and Chinese friends, and have tried to remain China hands for life. Hong Kong, for example, contains a large number of Westerners who no longer wish to return home. These are a valuable source of cultural and business information.

Reentry Issues

The return home following a foreign tour of duty is often accompanied by a number of problems. In many countries, expatriates enjoy higher standards of living than they do at home. Tax advantages, various bonuses, and weak local currencies often result in higher disposable incomes. Upon returning home, many employees find that resuming a more normal standard of living is a shock. This is especially true when the host country offers cheaper housing, inexpensive servants, and so forth.

This aspect of reentry is not an especially great problem for those on assignment in China, however. Working and living in China in many ways entails hardships, and few expatriates enjoy a quality of life higher than that of their home country. In this respect, the only problem upon return is boredom, if the expatriate and family members found their stay in China exciting, which many do.

Most expatriates, unless they have become totally immersed in Chinese culture or have become career China specialists, are happy to return home. The only personal advantages they have gained, aside from their experiences, are the financial bonuses and tax advantages given those who accept long-term assignments.

Reentry, however, poses a number of problems common to all returning expatriates, irrespective of the degree they enjoyed their foreign assignments. The returned employees usually must be reintroduced to corporate networks and office politics. In their absence, many colleagues and superiors will have changed positions or departed, and new individuals have joined the firm. Former expatriates usually find that their experiences and hard-won knowledge are unappreciated by others, and they have a sense of being forgotten and ignored.

Returnees can feel that their foreign experiences are valuable by becoming part of the training process for future expatriates. Each returnee should be assigned to other employees who expect to go on assignment in China. Returned expatriates can be asked to develop guides for prospective overseas employees. In this way, experience and personal knowledge are passed on and officially acknowledged as important and appreciated.

Mentoring and personal involvement in training programs by returning expatriates has another benefit. The Chinese prefer to conduct business with those they know. They dislike dealing with strangers. The mentoring process includes passing on names, recommendations, and letters of introduction. This provides the newly arrived expatriate with already functioning social networks of host culture nationals and fellow expatriates.

The Chinese are likely to prejudge a newcomer on the basis of their experiences with other Americans or representatives of the firm. It usually takes time to establish good working relationships, and a mentor-trainee link greatly shortens this period of adjustment. On the other hand, a failed relationship continues from one person to another. Thus some newcomers are labeled "ugly Americans," and their work is made more difficult without their knowing the reason.

Companies with an expected long-term presence in China can also form national or international networks made up of members with experience in China. Such interfirm and intrafirm networks provide valuable information for future projects and increase the self-worth of former China expatriates. A convention of China hands, sponsored by a firm or industry on an annual or semiannual basis, also maintains channels of communication.

Returning to the home country offers another "reverse culture shock" in terms of the returnee's work. Because overseas operations are generally understaffed, expatriates in China not only work long hours, but their work-related responsibilities are greater than those at home. Being successful in China demands a wide variety of skills, such as teaching and diplomacy.

Upon return, however, former expatriates usually experience the loss of responsibility and autonomy and a corresponding loss of their self-esteem. In China they enjoyed greater autonomy with fewer restrictions on how to achieve their work goals. Suddenly, they find themselves in a much more restrictive work environment. In fact, the very personality traits that make expatriates successful in China—adaptability, autonomy, self-confidence and patience—may result in frustration in the more bureaucratic and settled environment at home. In addition, homesickness and culture shock during the foreign assignment may have encouraged an expatriate to idealize work and the work environment in the home country. It is easy to become quickly disillusioned when reality sets in.

The practical result, in terms of former expatriates who have worked in China and elsewhere, is a tendency to change employers. The dropout rate of returned personnel has been estimated to be as high as 24 percent. There is a need to reduce this reverse culture shock through careful mentoring and other forms of organizational support.

European multinationals tend to make foreign assignments part of the normal career paths of management. No one can reach the higher managerial levels without having successfully experienced several foreign tours. This is especially true for European banks wishing to maintain a global presence. The European practice is to promote former expatriates as soon as they return. This policy gives returnees a reward for foreign assignments. It also offers new challenges and responsibilities at a time when reverse culture shock makes them unhappy with their former work. American multinationals could also benefit from this European strategy: former expatriates upon return from China (and elsewhere) should be given a promised promotion and, at a minimum, a change of duties.

Resentment by Peers

Colleagues often both envy and resent returnees. The returnee has been away for several years and has been out of touch. For many peers, returnees are viewed as strangers returning from exotic places, often with close ties to superiors. Expatriates perform unique services for the firm and deal with high-level officials that they would ordinarily seldom meet in a more normal assignment. In fact, many returnees have more contacts with higher officials only because they escorted them on foreign visits and reported directly to whatever executive was interested in the success of the foreign assignment.

Resentment and envy can be reduced by instant promotion or job rotation of the employee upon return from a foreign assignment. This reduces interpersonal conflict at a time of adjustment and growing disillusionment. The promotion also places envious peers out of reach, making their complaints suddenly sound like irrelevant sour grapes. The expectation of a promotion after a foreign tour also makes a foreign assignment more attractive.

To ease returnees' reverse cultural shock, Bechtel Group, Inc. asks employees who expect to end their foreign assignments in six months to list what they would most like to do when they return. The returnees are then given one of their top choices of work assignments, promotions, or both. This policy attracts the more ambitious to volunteer for foreign posts.

Retraining

A tour of duty in China does not offer much opportunity for reading trade journals or keeping up with current business trends. Although employees have gained valuable knowledge of foreign operations, they may find that some of their technical skills have become obsolescent. Companies might offer such employees the opportunity and time to enroll in training programs. Former expatriates are adaptable and willing to learn, and another opportunity to learn will be welcomed. This policy does, however, lengthen the time for total adjustment and a return to normalcy.

Endnotes

1. Allan Bird and Roger Dunbar, "Getting the Job Done Over There: Improving Expatriate Productivity," *National Productivity Review*, 10 (Spring): 45–56.
2. For an annotated review of the literature dealing with expatriate selection and the expatriate experience, see Jon P. Alston, *The Social Dimensions of International Business: An Annotated Bibliography* (Westport, Connecticut: Greenwood Press, 1993), chapter 3.
3. Ingemar Torbiorn, *Living Abroad: Personal Adjustment and Personnel Policy in the Overseas Setting* (New York: Wiley, 1982).
4. Ghislaine Hubbard, "How to Combat Culture Shock," *Management Today* (September 1986): 62–65; Rosalie L. Tung, "Corporate Executives and Their Families in China: Their Need for Cross-cultural Understanding in Business," *Columbia Journal of World Business* (Spring 1986): 21–25.
5. C. Carl Pegels, *Management and Industry in China* (New York: Praeger, 1987).
6. Dudley L. Poston, Jr., Michael Xinxiang Mao, and Mei-Yu Yu, "The Global Distribution of the Overseas Chinese Around 1990," *Population and Development Review* 20 (September 1994): 631–45.

7. J. Stewart Black and Mark Mendenhall, "The U-Curve Adjustment Hypothesis Revisited: A Review and Theoretical Framework," *Journal of International Business Studies* 22, no.2 (1991): 209–224.
8. Nancy J. Adler, *International Dimensions of Organizational Behavior* (Boston: PWS–Kent, 1991).

For Further Reading

Casse, Pierre. *Training for the Multicultural Manager.* Washington, D.C.: Society for Intercultural Education Training and Research, 1982.

Goldenberg, Susan. *Hands Across the Ocean: Managing Joint Ventures with a Spotlight on China and Japan.* Boston, Massachusetts: Harvard Business School Press, 1988.

Janssen, Gretchen. *Women Overseas: A Christian Perspective on Cross-cultural Adaptation.* Yarmouth, Maine: Intercultural Press, 1989.

Kohls, L. Robert. *Survival Kit for Overseas Living.* Yarmouth, Maine: Intercultural Press, 1984.

Sinclair, Kevin with Iris Wong Po-yee. *Culture Shock: China.* Portland, Oregon: Graphics Arts Center Publishing Company, 1990.

APPENDIX

Addresses and Telephone Numbers for Business and Government Organizations in China and the United States

(Telephone Country Code for China is 86)

Note: Chinese telephone systems are changing rapidly and all numbers are subject to change. The Chinese embassy and consulates have available a "China Trade Directory with Updated Directories."

Business-oriented Organizations

American Chamber of Commerce
  in Beijing
CITIC Tower Suite 2007
22 Jianwai Avenue
100004 Beijing
Tel: 1 532 2491
Fax: 1 512 7345

American Chamber of Commerce
  in Shanghai
Shanghai Tower Suite 435
1376 Nanjing West Rd.
200040 Shanghai
Tel: 21 279 8056
Fax: 21 279 8802

Bank of America N.T. & S.A.
Beijing Office Guesthouse 23
Qianmen Dong Dajie
Beijing, China
Tel: 55 2685
Telex: 22562 BKAME CN

Bank of China
410 Funei Avenue
100818 Beijing, China
Tel: 1 601 6688
Fax: 1 601 6869

Beijing International Trust and
    Investment Corporation
1 Chong Wenmenwai Dongdadi
Beijing
Telex: 223337 BITIC CN

Beijing Municipal Foreign Economic
    Relations and Trade Commission
3, First Lane,
South Lishilu
100045 Beijing
Tel: 1 866 511
Fax: 1 801 035

Business Research China
30 Salem Road
Weston, CT 06883 USA

Chamber of International
    Commerce, China
1 Fuwai Ave.
100860 Beijing
Tel: 1 851 3344
Fax: 1 851 1370

Chase Manhattan Bank N.A.
Rooms 1522 and 1524
Beijing Hotel
Beijing, China
Tel: 50 7766 1522
Telex: 22595 CHBJG CN

Chemical Bank
Beijing Representative Office
Room 105
Jianguo Hotel
Beijing, China
Tel: 50 2233 105
Telex: 22439 JGHBJ

China Association of Foreign-Owned
    Enterprises
18/F Section A
Poly Plaza
100027 Beijing
Tel: 1 500 1188
Fax: 1 501 9361

China Business Resources Co. Ltd
Room 3103, Hong Kong Plaza
188 Connaught Road West
Hong Kong
Tel: 852 2559 1399
Fax: 852 2540 8379

China Chamber of Commerce
4301 Connecticut Ave. NW Suite 136
Washington, DC 20008
Tel: 202 362-8462
Fax: 202 244-0478

China Tourism Administration
350 Fifth Ave Room 6413
New York, NY 10801
Tel: 212 760-9700

China United Trading Corporation
One World Trade Center Suite 3333
New York, NY 10048
Tel: 212 775-7079
Fax: 212 775-7273

Guangdong International Trust and
    Investment Corporation
4 Qiaoguang Road
Guangzhou, Guangdong
Telex: 44422 GITIC CN

Guangdong Provincial Foreign
    Economic Relations and Trade
    Commission
305, Donfeng Road Central
Guangzhou
510031 Guangdong, China
Tel: 20 343 985
Fax: 20 332 347

Japan External Trade Organization
1221 Avenue of the Americas
New York, NY 10020
Tel: 212 997-0400
Fax: 212 997-0464

Ministry of Commerce (MOC)
45 Funei Ave
100801 Beijing
Tel: 1 601-8518
Fax: 1 601-7209

Ministry of Finance (MOF)
Lane #3
Sanlihe South St.
100820 Beijing
Tel: 1 86 8731
Fax: 1 801 3428

Ministry of Foreign Economic
    Relations and Trade (MOFERT)
2 East Chang'an Ave.
100731 Beijing
Tel: 1 512-6644
Fax: 1 512-9214/9327

Office of the People's Republic of
    China and Hong Kong Affairs
International Trade Administration
U.S. Department of Commerce
Washington, DC 20230
Tel: 202 377-3583

People's Bank of China
32 Chengfang St.
100800 Beijing
Tel: 1 601 6491
Fax: 1 601 6724

Shanghai Investment and Trust
    Corporation
33 Zhongshan Dong Yi Road
Shanghai
Telex: 33031 SITCO CN

State Industry and Commerce
    Administration
8 Sanlihe East St.

100820 Beijing
Tel: 1 851 3300
Fax: 1 851 3394

The First National Bank of Chicago
Beijing Representative Office
Room 7022
Beijing Hotel
Beijing, China
Tel: 50 7766 7022
Telex: 22433 FNBC CN

Tianjin Municipal Foreign Economic
    Relations and Trade Commission
55, Chongquing Road
300050 Tianjin, China
Tel: 22 314 828
Fax: 22 316 640

US-China Business Council
Room 22/C
CITIC Tower
19 Jianwai Avenue
100004 Beijing
Tel: 1 500 2255 ext 2263, 2266
Fax: 1 512 5854

US-China Business Council
1818 N St. NW
Suite #500
Washington, DC 20036
Tel: 202 429-0340
Fax: 202 775-2476

Yunan Commission on Foreign Trade
    and Economic Cooperation
Foreign Trade Bldg.
576 Beijing Road
Kunming 650034
Tel: 871 312 8175
Fax: 871 313 3669

Major Chinese Companies and Other Organizations in the United States

Air China
45 East 49th St
New York NY 10017
Tel: 212 371 1349
Fax: 212 935 7951
Business: Air cargo and passenger
    transport

Bank of China NY Branch
410 Madison Ave.
New York, NY 10017
Tel: 212 935 3101
Fax: 212 593 1831
Business: Banking and financial

Ceroilfood New York, Inc.
2160 North Central Road 2–F
Fort Lee, NJ 07024
Tel: 201 461-3174
Fax: 201 461-3578
Business: Agricultural and food
   products

China American Insurance Co., Ltd
70 Pine St.
New York, NY 10270
Tel: 212 770-7862
Fax: 201 633-8336
Business: Insurance

China Arts/Crafts (USA)
300–3D Route 17 South
Lodi, NJ 07644
Business: Arts and crafts items

China Commodity Inspection Corp
   (CICC)
2341 205th Suite 113
Torrance, CA 90501
Tel: 310 787-9684
Fax: 310 787-9712
Business: Commodity Inspections; trade
   consultation

China Construction (USA) Inc.
One World Trade Center Suite 2949
New York, NY 10048
Tel: 212 488-8964
Fax: 201 777-1180
Business: Construction; real estate
   development; trading

China Meheco (USA) Inc.
1044 Road 23 Suite 102
Wayne, NJ 07470
Tel: 201 633-6603
Fax: 201 633-8336
Business: Medical and health products

China Resources Products (USA),
   Ltd.
225 West 34th St. Suite 610
New York, NY 10122
Tel: 212 629-4343
Fax: 212 629-6165
Business: General merchandise

China Silk America, Inc.
498 7th Ave. 24–F

New York, NY 10018
Tel: 212 465-9479
Fax: 212 465-1223
Business: Silk yarn; fabric and garments

China Sports of Norinco
2029 South Business Pkwy
Ontario, CA 91761
Tel: 909 923-1411
Fax: 909 923-0775
Business: Sports equipment; bicycles;
   motorcycles

China United Trading Corp.
One World Trade Center Suite 3333
New York, NY 10048
Tel: 212 775-0048
Fax: 212 775-7176
Business: General merchandise

ChinaTex America Inc.
209 West 40th St.
New York, NY 10018
Tel: 212 719-3250
Fax: 212 575-2013
Business: Garments

CITIC Representative Office
Two World Trade Center Suite 2250
New York, NY 10048
Tel: 212 938 0416
Business: Investments

Economist Intelligence Unite, The
The Economist Building
11 West 57th St.
New York, NY 10019
Tel: 212 554-0600
Fax: 212 586-1181
Business: Consultants

Heberican Intl. Inc.
525 Stuyvesant Ave.
Lyndhurst, NJ 07071
Tel: 201 933 7061
Fax: 201 933 6375
Business: General merchandise

International Pacific Exhibition, Inc.
133–139 Canal St.
New York, NY 10002
Tel: 212 219-9325
Fax: 212 219-9337
Business: Trade promotions and
   expositions

International Strategic Alliances, Inc.
1265 Montecito Ave. Suite 109
Mountain View, CA 94043
Tel: 415 969-1671
Fax: 415 969-1673
Business: Consultants

J.R.I. International
302 Irving St. Suite 716
San Francisco, CA 94122
Tel: 415 564-0215
Fax: 415 564-1879
Business: Consultants

Pacific & China Tours
60 East 42nd St. Suite 1061
New York, NY 10165
Tel: 212 867-2691
Fax: 212 661-5736
Business: Trade and package tours

Pecusa Co., Ltd
One World Trade Center Suite 2775
New York, NY 10048
Tel: 212 321-9460
Fax: 212 321-9467
Business: Petroleum and chemicals

Sumec Intl Inc.
23707 Batey Ave.
Harbor City, CA 90710
Tel: 213 326-5402
Fax: 213 326-8417
Business: Machinery and equipment

Sunry Import/Export Inc.
Paramus Plaza 2 Suite 125
120 Route 17–N
Paramus, NJ 07652
Tel: 201 967-7320
Fax: 201 967-0903
Business: Native products; tea; animal
    by-products

U.S. Embassy and Consulates in China

Embassy of the United States of
    America
2 Xiushui East St.
Beijing 100600

U.S. Consulate General in Chengdu,
    Sichuan
Jinjiang Hotel West Wing
1 Chendu
610012 Sichuan
Tel: 28 222 ext. 3141
Fax: 28 886 2341

U.S. Consulate General in
    Guandgong
White Swan Hotel
1 Shamian South St.

Guangzhou
510133 Guandong
Tel: 20 886 8911
Fax: 20 886 2341

U..S. Consulate General in
    Shenyang, Liaoning
40 Lane #4 Section #5
Sanjing St.
110003 Shenyang
Liaoning

U.S. Consulate General in Shanghai
1469 Huaihai Central Rd.
200031 Shanghai

Commercial Representatives of the Chinese Government in the United States

Commercial Office
Embassy of China
2300 Connecticut Ave. NW

Washington, DC 20008
Tel: 202 328-2520 ext. 27
Fax: 202 232-7855

Commercial Office
Consulate General of China
520 12th Ave.
New York, NY 10036
Tel: 212 330-7427
Fax: 212 502-0248

Commercial Office
Consulate General of China
1450 Laguna St.
San Francisco, CA 94115
Tel: 415 563-4858
Fax: 415 563-0494

Commercial Office
Consulate General of China
510 Shatto Pl. Suite 300
Los Angeles, CA 90020
Tel: 213 380-0587
Fax: 213 380-1961

Commercial Office
Consulate General of China
104 S. Michigan Ave. Suite 900
Monroe Bldg.
Chicago, IL 60603
Tel: 312 580-7403
Fax: 312 580-7402

Commercial Office
Consulate General of China
3417 Montrose Blvd.
Houston, TX 77006
Tel: 713 524-4064
Fax: 713 524-7656

INDEX

DATE DUE

1/22/2000			
MAR 1 9 2000			
JUN 1 8 2003			
JUN 2 4 2005			
APR 1 1 2007			
FEB 0 4 2010			
GAYLORD			PRINTED IN U.S.A.